S. R Wood

Immanuel

A Life of Jesus the Christ

S. R Wood

Immanuel
A Life of Jesus the Christ

ISBN/EAN: 9783337027575

Printed in Europe, USA, Canada, Australia, Japan

Cover: Foto ©Lupo / pixelio.de

More available books at **www.hansebooks.com**

IMMANUEL:

A LIFE OF JESUS THE CHRIST.

[FOR YOUNG PEOPLE.]

—BY—
REV. S. R. WOOD.

FERNDALE, HUMBOLDT COUNTY, CAL.
MATTHEWS & WOOLDRIDGE, PUBLISHERS.
1894.

To the young men and the young women of our land, this little volume is affectionately dedicated, with the hope that to some one of these it may bring a new conception of the Saviour.

AUTHOR'S NOTE.

The purpose the writer had in view in preparing this work was to put certain events in the life of Jesus in such a form as to lead young people to read them. If all our young people were Bible readers such an effort as this would be entirely unnecessary. The writer's earnest prayer is that those who read these pages may be induced to read and study carefully the pages of the Word containing a record of the events here referred to. It is also his prayer that each one who reads this little work will see Jesus in a new light and find in Him the dearest and best Friend, for, of a truth, He is IMMANUEL: "God with us." With this prayer was the work undertaken.

S. R. W.

Ferndale, California.

IMMANUEL.

CHAPTER 1.

Beneath the shade of a spreading willow in a very beautiful spot on the bank of the River Jordan, sat two young men. They were Hebrews, Bar-elah and Eliab, by name. Evidently the conversation in which they were engaged was an exceedingly interesting one.

The Jordan at this point presented a very beautiful appearance. The banks were thickly covered with trees. Great spreading willows were to be seen in abundance—occasionally there was an oleander in full bloom and now and then a tamarisk. Birds flitted about among the branches over head. The waters of the River were clear and cool and several times had the two young men thought of plunging, for a refreshing bath, into the deep hole near at hand.

The two young men before us were both of devout Jewish families. Their home was in the little village situated about an hour's journey from the spot where we find the two resting. In this village Bar-elah had been raised from infancy and to this village Eliab had come some two years before. Eliab was the older of the two; rather small of statue but well proportioned, and the twenty-two summers that had passed since he had first seen the light, had given him a darker complexion than his friend had. Eliab loved Bar-elah as he loved no other. The very sight of his friend filled him with delight and among the most blessed hours of his life were those when he communed alone with him.

Bar-elah was a sturdy youth of eighteen, much taller than his companion and finely formed—a magnificent specimen, physically, of God's handiwork; a handsome body, a handsomer face.

Eliab was a devout Hebrew youth, attending regularly at all the Synagogue services—and interested in all religious matters. Bar-elah was the opposite—indifferent, negligent, almost never entering a synagogue unless in company with Eliab.

The former had been away from his home on a rather adventurous journey for his father, and had only just returned on the morning of the day when we find him with Eliab on the river bank. The latter had sought the very first opportunity to be alone with his friend and had induced him to walk over to the river that they might be alone and commune together.

"My dear Bar-elah," spoke Eliab, "I'm so glad you're home with us again, I have much to speak to you of. There have been some wonderful occurrences since you left us. One John the Baptist, thought by some to be the Christ, went all through this country about Jordan preaching that men should repent of their sins, 'for,' said he, 'the Kingdom of Heaven is at hand,' and great throngs of people went out to hear him and many of them he baptized in the Jordan. Why Elah" for this was Eliab's favorite name for his friend, "I heard one day of this wonderful man and thought I to would go and see and hear him—and so I went expecting to see some one resembling some of our teachers, but lo! a man of uncouth appearance, with a raiment of coarse camel's hair and a girdle of skin about his loins. Some said he resembled greatly our prophet of old—Elijah. But his preaching was powerful. And I saw Publicans and Pharisees and Sadducees and numbers of others baptized of him in Jordan, confessing their sins. He told us though of one who was to come after him, who was mightier than he, who would baptize men with the Holy Ghost."

"And I am told that one day when he was thus preaching and baptizing, there came one who is called Jesus, to him, to be baptized of him. And shortly after, John saw this one called Jesus, who hails from Nazareth, and pointing to him he said: 'Behold the Lamb of God, which taketh away the sin of the world.'"

During all of Eliab's conversation he had had Bar-elah's undivided attention for all this was news to him. He had had no opportunity to hear what was going on in his own land during his trip for his father.

"Where is this one called Jesus, now, Eliab? I'd like to see him. I wonder if he is not the one of whom I heard as I came along the Jordan on my way home. We stopped a few moments to quench our thirst and found a curious old man on the bank of the river who was trying to explain something to a boy with him. All I heard was something about a place in the river, towards which the old man pointed, and I heard him say, 'there is where he was baptized. I was among the number who saw it all. And oh! such a beautiful, divine countenance.'"

"It must have been he, Elah," answered Eliab. "And do you know that we happened to be talking about these events at home this morning, just before you came—and I heard my good mother tell of some events that occurred when she and father were first betrothed. She said that she remembered very well hearing her people tell of a singular star that made its appearance one night and abode over the little town of Bethlehem. At the same time three strange looking magi came from the East and went first to Jerusalem and enquired at the city gates as to where they could find 'he that is born King of the Jews, for' said they 'we have seen his star in the east, and are come to worship him.' And upon hearing of this strange inquiry Herod gathered the Chief Priests and

Scribes together and found from them that the Christ should be born in Bethlehem of Judæa and he sent the magi to Bethlehem and as they were leaving the holy city the wonderful star made its appearance again to them and went before them until it stood over the place where the young child, whom they sought, was."

"Yes Eliab, I have heard my good mother tell of the same strange occurrences. And I remember hearing her tell that before this visit of the magi, the birth of this child was announced by an angel to some lowly shepherds on the plains of Bethlehem," answered Bar-elah.

"And do they think," continued Bar-elah, who had become by this time, thoroughly interested—"that this one is the Messiah so long looked for by Israel?"

"Yes, many already believe him to be the one who shall deliver Israel, Elah," answered Eliab.

The conversation between the two young men continued in this line for some time. At length the two started for their homes, Eliab the meanwhile rehearsing to his friend all that he had heard about this wonderful person, whom it was claimed was the Christ.

As they neared the village their thoughts turned to the approaching celebration of the Passover.

"How soon do you expect to leave to attend the Passover, Eliab?" asked Bar-elah.

"Probably in the course of three or four days, Elah—and say, Elah—you go when I do, will you?"

"All right Eliab I will," readily responded the other. "Do not our families plan to go together, anyway?"

"Yes, I believe they do, and say, Elah, I was just thinking, perhaps we will be able to see this one who is called Jesus—for if he is a faithful Israelite he must needs attend the great Feast," suggested Eliab.

"That's so Eliab and I'd like to see him, too."

The days that intervened between the above conversation between the two boys and the day on which their people had decided to set out for Jerusalem, were busy ones—days of preparation in which everything must be made ready for the journey and for the feast.

On the evening of the day before the start was to be made—Bar-elah went over to spend a quiet hour with Eliab. They repaired to the house-top where all was quiet and where they might talk without disturbance.

When they were settled comfortably, Bar-elah spoke:

"O Eliab, my brother Eleazar just returned to-night from Cana of Galilee and he tells us that there is great excitement up there about this Jesus of Nazareth. He says that not long ago there was a marriage feast up there and Jesus with some of his followers—his disciples—were at the feast, and during the festivities it was found that the supply of wine had been exhausted and this Jesus made wine out of water.

"Eleazar says, that they told him, and one of our cousins was a guest at the feast—this cousin I believe told Eleazar—that this Jesus saw six large waterpots of stone, and he directed the servants to fill these to the brim with water—just common water, and then directed them to draw out the water and lo! it was wine! At first some thought it was done through fraud but that couldn't be for the servants themselves testify that they knew not what was to happen and nothing was put into the water—and as far as I can learn Jesus did not as much as put his finger upon the waterpots. Surely this is the most astonishing miracle that I've heard of in my day."

"Truly that was marvelous. My dear Elah, we must see this one if we can," was Eliab's answer.

CHAPTER II.

EARLY on the morrow, among the companies that set out from the little village where Bar-elah and Eliab lived, was one company containing the two families to which these boys—or young men, belonged. There were just twelve in the party.

It was a most beautiful spring morning. The roadside was lined with bright flowers, the fields on either side were fresh and green and were flecked with gaily colored flowers.

It was not long before large numbers of travelers were to be seen along the road—all of them bound for Jerusalem to attend the great feast.

Although the women and children were not obliged to go up to the feast at this time, yet the entire families to which our two young men belonged, had turned out—Bar-elah's father and mother, three brothers, sister and himself, and

Eliab's widowed mother, two brothers, sister and himself. And it was a merry company too. It was a season for great rejoicing on the part of all devout Jews because of the mighty deliverance commemorated by the feast, and although some of the young people of the company did not feel as truly thankful as perhaps they ought to have, yet they seemed to catch some of the spirit of thankfulness manifested by their elders—and altogether it was an exceedingly happy company.

The seven young men of the company were afoot while the other five of the party rode on asses. Occasionally a pause would be made beneath some spreading sycamore, or at a spring.

At mid-day a short rest was taken in a very beautiful spot by the road-side, beneath a giant oak. There was some need of haste in order to reach the Holy City before the close of the day, for Bar-elah's people had as yet no place selected in which to prepare the Passover. Eliab's people were to go to the home of his uncle.

Toward evening the gate of the City was reached. Already large numbers of people had arrived and the roads approaching the City were thronged and crowds were about the gates.

"Elah," spoke up Eliab, as the company passed through the gate into the City—"mother thinks that our uncle can accommodate our whole company at his place—at least if you and I are willing to sleep upon the house-top together, and I guess we can agree to that can't we?"

"Most certainly we can Eliab. Three years ago the company we were with was late in arriving and had to pitch a couple of tents in order to find a place to stay, but this year we are early. And say Eliab, how do you plan to use the days between now and the feast? But then we can talk that over later. My what crowds there are already! It seems to me I never saw so many people before. I wonder if he who is called Jesus is here yet."

Upon arrival at the house of Japhlet—for this was the name of Eliab's uncle—room was found for the entire company, provided Eliab and Bar-elah took to the house-top, which proviso they readily agreed to.

That night after retiring Bar-elah renewed his question of the evening: "How do you plan to use the next few days, Eliab?"

"Well Elah, I've been thinking that we

might look about the City—visit the market-place, the bazaars, and the like, and the temple—and then too, it will be interesting to watch the crowds and who knows but what we may have an opportunity to see this Jesus of Nazareth. Then too, we will probably find many of the young men of our town and others whom we know and a whole party of us can go over to Gethsamane and to the Mount of Olives."

The days before the Passover passed just as Eliab had suggested. Old acquaintances were found, not only among those who dwelt in Jerusalem but among those who came from the other parts of the land of the Jews. Many a quiet hour did our two young men spend together in Gethsamane, where beneath a giant olive they talked over events that had transpired during the time they had been separated. Frequent references were made to the Christ for there was a desire on the part of each boy to see Him. On the part of Bar-elah, it was probably nothing more than mere curiosity, but on the part of Eliab, there was a feeling that possibly after all this one might be the one that some claimed Him to be, the long-promised, the long-looked for, the long-prayed for Messias.

One morning just before the opening of the feast, Eliab awoke first and while waiting for Bar-elah to awake he thought of various plans for the day, but the one that seemed to impress him most favorably, included a visit to the temple. As soon as Bar-elah awoke Eliab made known his plans and they were readily agreed to.

A few hours later found the two young men standing side by side within the sacred enclosure. There were many other visitors for by this time the City was crowded with people from the other parts of the land. Most of the people seemed to be about the court in which those were to be found, who dealt in sheep and oxen and doves for the temple sacrifices. These dealers were kept busy disposing of their stock to those who desired the animals for sacrifice. Numerous changers of money were found in this court, these too did a brisk business changing the various coins brought in by the people from outside of Jerusalem, into the half-shekel of the sanctuary. All was bustle and confusion. Men jostled against one another as they passed from stall to stall. The bleating of the sheep and the lowing of the cattle and the rattle of the money was accompanied by the shouting of dealers—and all this within the enclosure which had been solemnly dedicated to Jehovah.

Our two young men stood silently together taking in the scene when suddenly there was great confusion among the dealers and their cattle—and there was a general scattering. Upon their looking to ascertain the cause of all this, the boys saw one—Himself a young man, having a scourge of cords or rushes in His hand—and as they looked they saw Him drive the sellers of the oxen and sheep out of the temple and then turning to the money changers He caused their money to be poured out and then He overthrew their tables. Then to those that sold doves He said, with authority: "Take these things hence; make not my Father's house an house of merchandise."

Some of the Jews who saw what had been done, at once demanded of him the authority by which He had thus purged the temple. His answer to their question was:

"Destroy this temple and in three days I will raise it up."

His answer astonished the Jews for said they: "Forty and six years was this temple in building and wilt thou rear it up in three days?"

Bar-elah and Eliab were interested spectators of all these occurrences—but the querry with each was as to whom this one could be—this one who had assumed suddenly so much authority, certainly He was not of the Priests. The face attracted them, for while they could see the evidences there of the anger that was felt because of the gross sacrilege that had so long been permitted, still the boys saw a face of singular, divine beauty. As He passed from the court followed by a little company who seemed to be His followers —Bar-elah ventured to ask one of the number as to whom this young man might be.

"Jesus of Nazareth," was all the response Bar-elah received, but it was enough. Eliab heard it as plainly as did his companion. It had a strange effect on both young men. The very words seemed to thrill Eliab. Never before had Bar-elah, apparently so indifferent to religious truth, looked so serious. All the boys could do was to stand and look at this one concerning whom they had heard but whom neither had ever seen before. And as they looked the face of the Christ seemed to grow more radiant and divine, until, finally Eliab drew his friend to him and said softly:

"Truly, Elah, this is He."

*   *   *   *   *   *

The Passover was observed in the usual manner by the families to which Eliab and Bar-elah belonged. On the afternoon of the 14th of the month, Eliab's uncle, Japhlet, representing the company gathered at his home to observe the Passover, took the paschal lamb into the court of the temple where it was killed and dressed. The blood was given to the Priests who sprinkled it on the altar, and the fat was burned upon the altar. During all of this the Levites sang the hymn of praise prescribed for this ceremony.

When Japhlet reached his home the lamb was at once made ready for roasting, and after the 15th day had commenced, that is, when it had become dark, the little company consisting of Eliab's uncle, aunt and five cousins, with the families to which Eliab and Bar-elah belonged—nineteen souls in all—this company gathered about the Passover-table and partook of the Passover-lamb, the bitter herbs, the unleavened bread and whatever else was provided.

Bar-elah listened more attentively than ever

before to the declaration of the meaning of the feast, as made by Japhlet during the progress of the Passover-meal. This declaration impressed Eliab more forcibly than ever. Was it because their eyes had just shortly before rested upon One whom some believed to be the Messias?

CHAPTER III.

After the days for the observance of the feast were fulfilled, the little company containing Bar-elah and Eliab returned to the little village from whence it had come.

The months that followed were spent quietly by our two young men, in their village homes—Eliab prosecuting his studies and Bar-elah assisting his father in the work connected with the little parcel of ground upon which they lived, and upon the produce of which they depended for their livelihood.

Nearly a year passed in this way. Nothing much was ever heard about Jesus. The village was not visited much by outsiders and little was heard regarding events at any distance.

Many an hour were the two friends to be found together talking earnestly about the few wonderful works of Jesus of which they had heard.

One evening they were sitting together upon the house-top watching the setting sun and chatting together when news was brought to Bar-elah's father which made it necessary for Bar-elah to start next morning for the city of Samaria.

"Say Eliab," said Bar-elah when his father had returned to the rooms below, "you go home and tell your mother that you're going with me to-morrow and then come stay with me and we'll get a good early start—start at the rising of the sun—will you my boy?"

"Oh, my dear Elah, I would so much like to go with you, but—" and Eliab thought a moment, —"all right Elah, I'll go," and with that he was off. In a few moments he returned with the few things he needed for his journey.

With the rising of the sun the two young men were on their way—each mounted upon an ass.

The journey was a pleasant one, but the boys felt glad, when after having been hindered somewhat on their journey—they arrived on the third day within sight of the city of Samaria. Neither boy had ever visited the city before. Bar-elah's father had never before, to his son's knowledge, had any dealings in the land of the despised

Samaritans. Every thing at first looked strange to them. Once in a great while a Jew would be seen but never as much as talking with a Samaritan.

As Bar-elah and Eliab neared the city they found by the road-side, a young man, to all appearances, a Samaritan, who was evidently in trouble. His beast of burden had become fractious or frightened and had spilt the pack from off its back and the young man was having a hard time trying to fix things. As the boys drew nearer they saw that he was struggling with a load that was really too much for him.

"Let's help him Elah, even if he is a despised Samaritan," suggested Eliab, for his heart had been touched after witnessing the fruitless efforts of the young man to right matters, and he really felt sorry for him.

Our two young men proffered their help which was gladly accepted and the young man was profuse with his thanks.

"I perceive that you are both Jews," said he as he eyed them from head to foot. "One of your people has created a great stir in some parts of our land. The whole city of Sychar is aroused because of his doings."

"Who is he and where does he hail from and what does he do that's wonderful—if you'll pardon so many questions," asked Eliab.

"Jesus of Nazareth," was the only response from the young Samaritan.

Bar-elah and Eliab looked at one another in astonishment. Was it possible that this One whom they had seen so zealous for the sacred temple of the Jews was now among the hated Samaritans?

And was it possible that they might again get a glimpse of that wonderfully attractive face?

The boys seemed to read one another's thoughts for they spoke not a word.

"We saw this One in Jerusalem at the great feast," spoke up Eliab, after a moment or two—"but had no hopes of finding Him here in Samaria."

"Oh he was merely passing through our land on his way to Galilee," explained the young Samaritan.

"But what great work has He been doing here in your land?" asked Bar-elah, and Eliab noticed a real evidence of interest on the part of his friend.

"Well," began the young Samaritan, "it seems he had been working or teaching down in Judæa

after he had attended the Passover of the Jews at Jerusalem, and then decided to go into Galilee, but instead of crossing the Jordan and going through Perea as so many of the Jews do, in order to avoid us, he, with some of his disciples, came right through our land to the city of Sychar. That is the place you know, near which Jacob's well is situated. He forthwith sent his disciples into the city to buy meat—and being weary and thirsty from his journey he sat on the well to rest. While he sat thus a woman came to draw water from the well—and he being thirsty asked her to give him to drink of the water she drew. His request astonished her and she could not refrain from giving expression to her astonishment—to think that he, a Jew, would ask drink of one who was a woman of Samaria, seeing the Jews had no dealings with the Samaritans. But her astonishment seemed the greater when he told her that he could give her to drink of living water and after drinking of it she would never thirst again.——
Said he: 'Whosoever drinketh of this water'—meaning that which the woman had drawn—'shall thirst again; but whosoever drinketh of the water that I shall give him shall never thirst;

but the water that I shall give him shall be in him a well of water springing up into everlasting life.' These are the words the woman repeated afterwards. Rather a queer statement is it not?

"But more than that—this man—and I afterwards learned that he is called Jesus of Nazareth —this one, as the woman afterwards testified to the men of the city, told her all things that ever she did. She was one who had done wickedly and he told her all about it. More than that, he declared himself to be the Messias.

"After this she went into the city and told the men all about the wonderful things that this one who claims to be the Messias, told her. The result was that large numbers went out of the city to where he was—and many of them believed on him. So many, in fact, that the Samaritans besought him to tarry with them a season and he did so—remaining for two days During that time many more of the city believed after hearing him speak. Some of them declaring him to be the Christ, the Saviour of the world."

"And is he still in Samaria?" asked Bar-elah who with Eliab, had given undivided attention to all the young Samaritan had told them.

"No," was the young man's reply. "After two days he went into Galilee. Of course I do not know as much about his doings there as I do of those nearer my home—for I too belong to Sychar. But my brother is among those who believe Jesus to be the Christ and he of course feels interested enough to keep posted on all that this one does and only yesterday he had from one who had come from Capernaum a full report of the wonderful things done there.

"This Jesus it seems has been teaching in their synagogues in Galilee and a fame of him went through all the country round about. It seems that one day he went to Cana in Galilee, where it is said, he had more than a year before, miraculously made wine out of water. A certain ruler or nobleman living in Capernaum and whose son was at the point of death, heard that Jesus was in Cana and went over to him and begged him to go down to Capernaum and heal his son— but instead of going, this Jesus simply said to him: 'Go thy way; thy son liveth.' And the ruler believed what he said and started for home. On the way he met his servants who were on their way to Cana to tell him that his son was better and upon inquiry it was found that at the very hour in which this Jesus had said 'thy son liveth,' the fever left him."

"Then," continued the young Samaritan, "he went to Nazareth, the city where he had been brought up and on the Sabbath day went into their Synagogue and opening the book of the prophet Esaias he read a prophesy concerning the Messias and expounded the Scriptures to the people and declared that that day that Scripture which he had read was fulfilled in their hearing. And the people wondered because of the gracious words that he spake but after a time they became so filled with wrath that they thrust him out of the city and took him to the brow of the hill, intending to cast him over, but he just quietly walked out from among them and went his way, and went down to Capernaum."

The relating of these occurrences excited both Bar-elah and Eliab with a greater desire than ever they had had before to see the Christ and to see some of His wonderful works. They had neither of them moved even so much as a finger while their newly made acquaintance had been rehearsing the doings of Jesus. Within the heart of Eliab there seemed to be a feeling that this one must, indeed, be the Messias. Bar-elah felt interested to a certain extent.

"Well where is He now?" asked Eliab.

"In Capernaum," answered the Samaritan—"But I must hasten on my journey," he continued and again he expressed his thanks to the boys for their help.

"I feel that we ought to thank you," was Eliab's response, "for we have heard a great deal from you that interests us Jews." And the two went on their way into the city while the Samaritan went his way along the country road.

"A fine face Elah," said Eliab referring to the young man.

"Kind of nice fellows, if they are Jews," said the young Samaritan to himself as he looked back at them—"and fine specimens of young manhood too."

CHAPTER IV.

BAR-ELAH attended to his father's business immediately upon arriving in the city of Samaria and as no hospitality was shown the Jews by the Samaritans, the boys concluded that their stay in the city would not be very pleasant hence they decided to leave at once and to sleep by the road-side on the way home, rather than stay in the city, and so at about the ninth hour they passed through the gates on their homeward journey. The nights were quite pleasant and not at all uncomfortable. During the interval between the interview with the young man of Samaria, and the hour for returning, both the boys seemed to be deeply engaged with their thoughts. Neither of them said very much. Eliab noticed that Bar-elah seemed especially serious.

It was a beautiful night. The moon shone

forth in all her glory. It was very light. After they had rolled themselves up in their cloaks for the night, Bar-elah, who lay close to Eliab's side, said:

"Eliab, don't you know I'd like to see more of this Jesus of Nazareth. I'd like to see him perform some of the miracles that are spoken of."

"Yes, my dear Elah," replied Eliab, raising himself partly and looking into the face he loved—"and I'd like to hear some of the gracious words that He speaks and feast my eyes on that divine countenance."

"Well I've done some thinking since our talk with that young Samaritan and I've a plan to suggest to you Eliab. It may be worth your thoughts for a while if worth nothing more. I was thinking that we might just as well go back to Capernaum for a while after we get home and spend a little time there—perhaps as long as Jesus remains there—and thus have an opportunity to see more of him. You know I have an uncle there and I know they'll make room for us and be glad to have us visit with them a while. What think you? Will you join me in this, Eliab?"

Eliab did not respond for a moment.

"Oh Eliab that's just what I have been wishing for many weeks, that we might do. Yes, of course I'll join you my friend. Capernaum, you know, was our home for some six or seven years and I have friends to whom we can go if need be."

"That's so—well we will go if you agree."

"I agree," responded Eliab heartily.

When the two young men reached their homes they at once made their plans known to their parents. At first Bar-elah's mother objected seriously to his going.

"Why," said she, "who knows what false prophet this one may be or whether or not he is possessed of a devil." But after being reminded of the fact that her son Bar-elah was by no means interested in religious matters and that it was probably nothing but mere idle curiosity that prompted him to plan this trip and the further fact that his companion Eliab was a thoroughly devout Hebrew—one who was in some respects one of the most promising ones of the faith —she felt that it probably would not hurt the boys to go.

"For," said she, "if there's anything bad about it Eliab will find it out and shield Bar-elah from its influences—and if there's anything good about it—I want them both to embrace it."

The two young men made hasty preparations for their journey and the next day saw them on their way—and they went right through Samaria too, not desiring to lose time by going by way of Perea—and too, they rather hoped that in the neighborhood of Sychar they might see again the young Samaritan whom they had befriended and from whom they had learned so many things regarding the Christ—but when Sychar was reached the young man was not to be seen.

They travelled more than an ordinary day's journey each day; "For," as Eliab had said, "we must reach Capernaum before the Sabbath and we must need make great haste." A few hours before the commencement of the Sabbath, Bar-elah knocked at the door of his uncle's house in Capernaum. The two young men were bidden enter and both were accorded a very hearty welcome.

When the Sabbath had come, in the cool of the evening, the two boys, as was their custom at home when together, went up to the house-top, there to commune.

"It occurred to me this evening Elah," said

Eliab, "that He who is called the Christ will surely worship at the Synagogue and that large numbers who have been negligent about attending will be there and we had better go early in order to get in for we must see the Christ as soon as we can."

Some little time before the appointed hour for service the people began to gather at the Synagogue, Bar-elah and Eliab among them. It was evident that when the time for the service to commence would arrive, the place would be well filled. Shortly before the services the young men noticed a movement on the part of the whole congregation and looking in the direction in which every eye was turned—the eyes of our young men rested upon the person of Jesus of Nazareth. And oh! such a radiance as was to be seen in that face! It seemed lighted with the glory of heaven. The boys did not take their eyes off of Him for an instant and Bar-elah found Eliab grasping his hand with a death-like grip.

But all stir was hushed in an instant when the solemn service began. Suddenly every eye was again turned toward the Christ as He slowly arose from His seat and assumed a position of authority. Every eye was fixed on Him; everything was as still as death; every ear was opened eager to hear the first word this wonderful man should speak. And when He spoke those who heard were astonished at His teaching, for He did not teach as did the Scribes, but as one who had authority. But suddenly there was an interruption and one was heard to cry out:

"Let us alone; what have we to do with thee, thou Jesus of Nazareth? art thou come to destroy us? I know thee who thou art, the Holy One of God."

Every eye was fixed upon the one who thus cried out and it was seen that he was one possessed with a spirit of an unclean devil. Then every eye was turned to Him of whom even the unclean spirit had testified that He was the Holy One of God. But He only quietly rebuked him, saying: "Hold thy peace, and come out of him." Then was witnessed a struggle as the unclean spirit tore the man and wrestled with him—but the devil obeyed the command and came out of the man and left him sound and well.

Amazement filled the people. With astonishment one was heard to say: "What thing is this?" Another asked, "What new doctrine is this? for," said they, "with authority commandeth he even the unclean spirits, and they do obey him."

Our two young men were as much astonished as were any. Never had they heard of such things; never had they seen anything like this.

"Truly, Elah," said Eliab slipping his arm about Bar-elah as they went forth from the Synagogue, "this must be the Christ, the Messias. And surely if He can cleanse a man of an evil spirit He can cleanse him of the evil that's within his heart."

Bar-elah was thoughtful and heard all his friend said, but he said nothing—the only evidence that he gave that he had heard his companion was the pressure he gave his hand.

As the people went forth from the Synagogue at the close of the services they carried the news of Christ's power everywhere until his fame spread throughout all Galilee. After He had gone out of the Synagogue He went to the home of one Simon, whose wife's mother was sick with a great fever. Jesus simply rebuked the fever and she who had been sick was immediately cured and arose from her couch and ministered unto

Jesus and His disciples who were with Him. The news of this miraculous cure at once spread everywhere about the city. Bar-elah and Eliab both heard of it. Towards the close of the Sabbath Bar-elah's uncle came to where the boys were siting in the garden and said to them:

"It would, perhaps, be well for you to go, at the setting of the sun down to Simon's house, for I hear that every one in the city who has a sick one is going to take that one down there to Jesus of Nazareth to be healed. Aged Mattaniah, who lives in the next house, infirm as he is, is planning to take his sick and crippled grandson—a fine young man, but oh, such a sufferer—he plans to have him carried down to this Jesus."

The uncle had no idea how welcome this news was to the boys. They at once said they would go that way and they immediately started. As they walked along they saw those who were diseased and even some who were possessed of devils, going or being taken towards the house of Simon. There were mothers carrying sickly babes in their arms. There were parents leading children having divers diseases. Young men who had lost all the brightness and life and bloom of youth—old men who were racked with disease—some of them walking with the help of staffs—some being led by friends, some being carried on beds—but all going in the one direction.

Our two young men had not gone far before they overtook aged Mattaniah as he trudged along beside the bed upon which lay the suffering young grandson. Bar-elah caught just one glimpse of the face and heard only one expression from the little party and that came as a moan from the sufferer. The face, though not beautiful, as the world uses the term, was to Bar-elah one of unusual attractiveness. The words that Bar-elah heard from the lips of the sufferer were these: "Oh, if he only can!" They touched Bar-elah, for he realized they meant a great deal.

The two boys hurried along. As they came in view of the house they could see that already a large crowd had gathered in front of the door.

"The whole city must be gathered there," said Bar-elah.

"It looks like it," replied Eliab. And it was the truth for ere long the whole city was gathered at the door. It was an anxious throng—anxious for the coming forth of the One who had already proven Himself to be the great physician.

The door opened and He came forth and oh, what compassion, what love, what mercy beamed in His very countenance! There was a stir in the throng as they all tried to get to Him with their loved ones who were diseased or possessed. The Christ simply laid His hands on the sick and they were healed. Mothers whose babes had been sick went away with hearts aglow with thanksgiving as they looked into the faces of the little ones who were now well and strong—simply through the touch of the Christ. Old men left their staffs behind, and walked off as briskly as in their youth. The diseased and tortured were restored to perfect health.

Our two young men looked on with amazement. Such strange and unheard of sights! They watched closely so as to see when aged Mattaniah went up to the Christ with his grandson.

"There he goes," whispered Eliab to Bar-elah. "See, they have reached the Christ."

For a moment He stood over the bed whereon the young man lay—then stretching forth His hand He touched him. The young man arose and stood before them all, perfectly restored.

Wonder of **wonders**! No more longings for health, no more torture of pain. Oh! wonderful touch! Oh blessed hand! Oh glorious Christ!

Then too, some **who** were possessed with devils were there, and by speaking **the** word, the Christ caused the evil spirits to come forth and as they did **so** they cried out with a loud voice:

"**Thou art** Christ the Son of God."

When Eliab heard this testimony his heart was thrilled for **he** felt a response there, for surely, thought he, **this** must be the Christ of God.

After the healing **and** when Christ had quietly retired from the **presence of the** multitude that thronged about the door—Bar-elah and Eliab started **for** the house of the uncle, and as **they** walked along they overtook aged Mattaniah **who** was now leaning upon the strong arm of his grandson Eliphaz. Oh! how different was it but a **short time** before when this same young man was tortured **with** pain and disease and was being carried by others through this same **street**! Bar-elah remembered the longing expressed **by** Eliphaz when he passed him on his way to the Christ.

The face that had appeared attractive to Bar-elah when first he saw it, was **doubly** so now, for the flush and life and beauty of youth had returned.

When the two young men had gone to their bed-chamber they sat together for some time talking about the events of the Sabbath and of the evening.

"My dear Elah," said Eliab, drawing closer to his friend, "I believe this Jesus is, indeed, the Messias. And it seems to me that One who can cleanse men of physical defilement can also cleanse men from all defilement because of sin. How pure and holy and Godlike He looks. I want to be like Him, Elah. I can't help but think of the wonderful change in the aged neighbor's grandson. Yes, this Jesus must be the Messias for whom we have looked so long."

Bar-elah made no response except to clasp his companion's hand in his own. Eliab knew that Bar-elah was thinking deeply.

As Eliab fell asleep he thought he heard again these words:

"Thou art Christ, the Son of God."

CHAPTER V.

To the great disappointment of Bar-elah and Eliab the stay of Jesus and His disciples in Capernaum was necessarily very short as He must needs go into the other cities of Galilee, and He did so, preaching in their Synagogues. The first thought of our young men was to follow the Christ for several of the town people had done so—but they were not able to depart from the city for several days. Those were anxious days for them both and it was with great joy that they hailed the morn on which they were able to take their departure from the city to follow the Christ.

After a long day's journey they found they were not far from where He was laboring among the people. They found that He had continued His great work of healing and that great numbers had been restored. They also found that great multitudes of people were following Him from one place to another—not only people from Galilee but also from Decapolis and from Jerusalem, and from Judæa, and from beyond Jordan.

The next day Bar-elah, with Eliab, stood once more in the presence of Jesus of Nazareth. A large number of people were following Him, anxious to hear every word that proceeded out of His mouth and to see everything that He did. Suddenly there was a scattering of the crowd—or rather an opening made through the midst of it as a man, full of leprosy, was seen approaching Jesus as hastily as he could. Every one drew back from him fearing, lest his garment should touch theirs and they thereby become defiled and possibly have that dreaded, that awful disease conveyed to them. No one sought to hinder his approach for no one dared touch him.

Bar-elah and Eliab looked on in wonder. Did this one who was making directly for the Christ—did this one intend to touch and thus defile the Christ? Every eye was upon him. Would the Christ get out of his way or suffer him not to come near Him?

But see—he falls on his face before Jesus—and what are those words he utters? Bar-elah and Eliab heard them.

"Lord, if thou wilt, thou canst make me clean." What will the Christ do? Can he cleanse one so terribly afflicted?

Those who looked into the face of the Christ saw there a look of wonderful compassion. And what is this He does? He stretches forth His hand and touches the leper and says to him:

"I will; be thou clean."

And straightway he was cleansed of his leprosy, and although Jesus charged him particularly that he was to tell no man of this, he who had been cleansed went out and published everywhere that he could, the news of his wonderful cleansing. The effect of this was that Jesus was unable to enter openly into the city—because of the immense multitudes that came to Him, but had to resort to desert places—and even there the people flocked to him from every quarter, Bar-elah and Eliab being among those who followed Him.

They heard that Jesus was soon to return to Capernaum and after some days followed by much people, He did so. Bar-elah and Eliab returned to the city also. It was soon noised abroad that Jesus was there and a great throng of people gathered about the house, so there was not room to enter.

Bar-elah and Eliab, however, arrived in time to secure an entrance and while there they saw another of Jesus' mighty works, for one sick with the palsy was brought and when those who bore him came to the house—for he was borne of four —they could not gain an entrance into the house so they went to the house-top and let the sick of the palsy down through the roof until he came before the spot where Jesus stood preaching the word to the multitude that had gathered about Him. And oh such wonderful and gracious words as He spake! Every one of them thrilled Eliab and as he fixed his eyes upon Jesus, as He spake, it seemed to Eliab that he must accept this One as the Messias, the Son of God.

The sick of the palsy lay before Jesus, looking piteously into the face so full of tenderness and love and compassion.

Jesus seeing their faith saith to the man: "Son, be of good cheer; thy sins be forgiven thee."

Immediately some of the scribes and Pharisees whispered among themselves, charging the Christ with blasphemy for presuming, as they thought, to forgive sins. But Jesus knew their thoughts, although He did not hear their murmurings, and He said to them: "Why reason ye these things in your hearts? Whether is it easier to say to the sick of the palsy, Thy sins be forgiven thee; or to say, Arise, and take up thy bed, and walk? But that ye may know that the Son of man hath power on earth to forgive sins, I say unto thee, Arise, and take up thy bed, and go thy way into thine house."

And the man arose in the presence of all of them, took up his bed, and walked away—a cured man—a perfectly restored man—and as he went he glorified God. And those who witnessed this wonderful cure, were amazed and many of them also, glorified God.

Not only did the words of Christ and the proof He gave the Pharisees, answer the questions in the hearts of the scribes and Pharisees—but they also answered a question in the heart of Eliab.

He had through the teachings of Christ which he had heard, been aroused to a sense of his need of forgiveness of sin and now the words he heard from those divine lips:

"That ye may know that the Son of man hath power on earth to forgive sins,"—and the evidence of this, made him feel that he too ought to become a disciple of the Christ and when alone with his companion he said to him:

"Elah, I believe that this Jesus of Nazareth is the Son of the living God—and that He has power to forgive sins and I purpose following Him."

Bar-elah made no audible reply, but Eliab read in his friend's face, as their eyes met, a response which he saw was not at all unfavorable to his plans.

"And, Elah," continued Eliab, "I mean to leave all and follow Him—but I want you my friend to go with me even if you do not feel just as I do about it."

"Well, I'll tell you, Eliab," answered Bar-elah, "while I don't feel at all as you do, I do want to go with you wherever you go. I haven't seen enough of him yet. But I don't want people to think I'm one of his followers for I don't feel exactly as you do, Eliab."

Eliab had truly been born anew and was now a son of God. His soul was filled with joy unspeakable, and the peace that passeth all understanding. He had found in Jesus the Great Physician who had power to heal the soul of all diseases.

His great concern now was for his own dear Elah. Oh! such a burden as rested upon his heart for this one whom he loved! and the thought last in his mind as he dropped off to sleep as he lay beside Bar-elah that night was, "Oh that I might bring my Elah, diseased with sin, to the blessed Christ, that He might touch him and heal him!"

CHAPTER VI.

THE time for the Passover drew nigh and again every road was filled with caravans of devout Jews, all headed towards Jerusalem, where they were going to attend the great feast. Jesus and His disciples were among those who went from Capernaum. Bar-elah, Eliab and Eliphaz, with whom our young men had now become well acquainted, were among those who went up to Jerusalem.

On the Sabbath day Jesus went to the pool of Bethesda, which is by the sheep gate, and there He found a great multitude of blind, withered, halt, diseased ones waiting until the water of the pool should be stirred, for at such times, when the waters would gush forth from the springs feeding the pool, it was held that at such times the curative properties of the pool were increased and then it was that all those lying in the porches surrounding the pool, would at once hurry into the water.

Jesus found one poor, lonely, helpless, infirm man, who could not drag himself down to the pool before the stirring of the water had ceased and others had crowded him out. This man had been infirm thirty and eight years and had during the time he had been there at the pool made repeated efforts to find relief, but all in vain.

Jesus saw this man and knowing his case full well approached him. Bar-eiah and Eliab stood near. Jesus said to the man: "Wilt thou be made whole?"

The poor man knew not who it was that spoke to him, but still depending entirely upon the waters of the pool for relief, explained to Jesus the difficulty of his getting into the water when it was stirred. But Jesus simply said to him:— "Rise, take up thy bed, and walk." And immediately he did so. Thereupon the Jews murmured against the man for he carried his bed on the Sabbath and according to their belief this was unlawful. The only defense the man put forth, however, was that this One who had made him whole had told him to take up his bed.

Afterwards in the temple Jesus revealed Himself to the man—and the man departed from the temple and told the Jews that it was Jesus who had healed him of his infirmity. Upon hearing this the Jews sought to persecute and slay Jesus, simply because He had made this man whole on the Sabbath day. Jesus answered the Jews at some length. In His discourse to them, among other blessed truths uttered was this :

"Verily, verily, I say unto you, He that heareth my word, and believeth on him that sent me, hath everlasting life, and shall not come into condemnation; but is passed from death unto life."

Oh! how those words thrilled Eliab's heart!

"Blessed, blessed words," thought he. "Just what I have experienced. O give thanks unto the Lord, I have passed from death unto life—condemnation no longer rests upon me." His face shone with the light that was in his soul.

"Eliab," said Bar-elah as they walked along the street a little later, "You seem so happy, why is it? I wish I could feel as bright as you do— why boy, your face literally shines, you are so happy."

"Oh Elah," replied Eliab slipping his arm through Bar-elah's, "it is my new found joy through believing in Jesus of Nazareth, the Christ, the Son of God. And oh! how I wish this joy was yours!"

They walked on in silence.

* * * * * *

After the feast of the Passover, Jesus returned to Galilee with His disciples. Eliab accompanied by Bar-elah, followed Him thither—and almost immediately after their arrival had another opportunity of seeing one of His wonderful works. It was the Sabbath and Jesus and His disciples had gone to the Synagogue. Bar-elah and Eliab were there. There was also in the Synagogue a man whose hand was withered. Jesus spoke to the man and told him to stand forth in the midst of them. He did so, and then after He had questioned the murmuring Jews as to whether or not it was lawful to do good on the Sabbath day and receiving no response from them—Jesus saith unto the man:

"Stretch forth thine hand,"—and to the amazement of every one the man stretched forth his withered, helpless, seemingly lifeless hand and it was fully healed and restored. Bar-elah looked at Eliab with amazement. Astonishment was written upon every line of his countenance. But some of the Jews present were filled with wrath and at once began, after they had gone out from the Synagogue, to counsel together against Jesus. Eliab's belief in Jesus was stronger than ever, while Bar-elah had to admit to his friend that:

"Surely it does seem as if this One must have been sent from God."

When Jesus knew of the plans of the Jews against Him, He at once quietly withdrew and went to the Sea of Galilee. Great multitudes followed Him, not only from Galilee but also from Tyre and Sidon and from beyond the Jordan, many of them diseased and all of them eager to touch Him, because of the virtue that came from Him and that cured their diseases and cast out their unclean spirits. As we might well expect, Bar-elah and Eliab were both among the people who thronged about Jesus.

When Jesus looked upon the multitude that had followed Him, He went up into a mountain and sat down to teach them. He uttered many wonderfully gracious words. Truths that thrilled the hearts of His hearers.

"Blessed are the poor in spirit:" said He, "for theirs is the kingdom of heaven. Blessed are they that mourn: for they shall be comforted. Blessed are the meek: for they shall inherit the earth. Blessed are they which do hunger and thirst after righteousness: for they shall be filled. Blessed are the merciful: for they shall obtain mercy. Blessed are the pure in heart: for they shall see God. Blessed are the peacemakers: for they shall be called the children of God."

Such statements as these, the multitudes had not heard from any other teacher.

"Ye are the salt of the earth:" said Jesus. "Ye are the light of the world."

"The salt of the earth," thought Eliab, as he repeated the words to himself.

"Salt preserves: salt heals. Can He mean that we who are His followers are to help to heal the sin-sick and diseased? Can He mean that we are to help keep the souls of men from putrefying?" And Eliab had a new conception of what it meant to be a follower of Jesus Christ. "The light of the world," thought he. "To help dispel the darkness of iniquity. Oh! what a glorious discipleship is this!"

Bar-elah listened with eagerness to every word that the Christ spoke. His eyes were fastened on the great teacher. Not once during the entire discourse were they removed, such was his attention and interest.

"Be ye therefore perfect, even as your Father which is in heaven is perfect," said Jesus.

"Yes," thought Eliab, "that is the longing of my heart: to be perfect as this One the Christ, is —as the Father in heaven is."

Many other wonderful teachings followed:

"Lay not up for yourselves treasures upon earth, where moth and rust doth corrupt, and where thieves break through and steal: but lay up for yourselves treasures in heaven, where neither moth nor rust doth corrupt, and where thieves do not break through nor steal: For where your treasure is, there will your heart be also."

And as he heard these words Bar-elah was forcibly reminded of the great loss his father had once suffered, when one night, unknown to all the family, a thief had broken into the little chest where all their earnings were stored, and made away with them all, leaving the family with nothing. The words of Christ impressed him forcibly.

And many other wonderful words spake Jesus to the multitude gathered before Him, the result being they were all filled with astonishment at His doctrine and manner of teaching.

As they came down from the mountain Eliab slipped his arm about Bar-elah, saying as he did so:

"My dear Elah, have you ever heard such wonderful truths? Do you not believe too, that this One is, indeed, the Christ of God?" Bar-elah was silent. "It seemed to me Elah," continued Eliab, "that I never had the truth impressed on me more forcibly. Just think Elah, of such statements as we heard from His gracious lips: 'Seek ye first the kingdom of God, and his righteousness;'—His righteousness remember, not our own—'and all these things shall be added unto you.' And what a glorious promise that; 'Ask, and it shall be given you; seek, and ye shall find; knock, and it shall be opened unto you.'

"Then too, what He said about the strait gate that leads to life and the wide gate that leads to destruction. Elah, I believe I have, through this Christ, entered the strait gate. Dear Elah, will you not believe on Him also?"—pleaded Eliab. Bar-elah was silent for a moment and then taking Eliab's hand in his own, he said:

"Eliab, I want more time to think about these things. But I'll tell you my boy, I never realized how ungodly I was until I compared my life with the pure, unspotted, holy life of Jesus."

Eliab's heart bounded with joy for he felt that Bar-elah must certainly be coming to the light.

As the multitude separated for the time being, our young men suddenly found themselves face to face with Eliphaz, the young man of Capernaum whom they had seen healed by Jesus.

"Eliphaz," said both boys at the same time as they looked with astonishment into his attractive face,—"are you here, too?"

"Yes," said Eliphaz after their more formal greetings were over,—"I was one of the number to follow this one called Jesus, from Capernaum. He says some wonderful things, does He not?"

"But say, Bar-elah and Eliab, come abide with me to-night, at my cousin's home?"

The three young men spent some time together discussing the teachings of the Christ and were just settled for the night when a messenger came to the house to summons Eliphaz to the death-bed of a very intimate friend—a young man in the city of Nain.

"Well, Eliab and Bar-elah," said Eliphaz as he came into the room where the two boys had been asleep, "I shall have to leave you. One whom I have long known and loved is sick unto death and he wants to see me. I fear that even now I am too late for the messenger left yesterday at the rising of the sun and was delayed on the way and too, he had trouble finding me. I fear my friend has already died. So I must needs make haste. The Lord be gracious to you until we meet again."

CHAPTER VII.

THE day after, Jesus with a number of His disciples and many people, Bar-elah and Eliab among the number, went into the city of Nain.

"Is not Nain the city to which Eliphaz went, Eliab?" asked Bar-elah, as they came in sight of the city.

"Yes," replied Eliab.

"What means that crowd of people coming through the gate of the city, Eliab?" asked Bar-elah as he saw a large number of people approaching.

"Why, Elah, I believe it is one being taken to the burial," answered Eliab. "I wonder," said he turning quickly to his friend as a sudden thought seemed to come to him, "I wonder if it can be that the friend of Eliphaz is dead!"

The funeral procession was a long one. The two multitudes—the one following the body of the dead, and the one following Jesus—met. Barelah soon recognized Eliphaz among the chief mourners and from this he knew that the body was that of the young man whom Eliphaz had gone to visit. Eliab too, saw **Eliphaz**.

The mother of the young man walked close beside the body of her boy. Her grief was intense for not only had she lost her boy, but in losing him she had had her only support taken away,—for he was her only son and she was a widow. When Jesus saw her His heart was touched. It was filled with compassion. He approached her. Every eye was on Him. What would He say, what would He do? Eliphaz was quick to recognize Him and his heart bounded with delight when he saw the face so full of compassion and love, the face of the One who had done so much for him. Could He help him now in his grief?

When **He came** to the griefstricken mother, He simply said to her: "Weep not,"—and then turning to the bier whereon the young man's body lay, He touched it and the bearers of it stood still and Jesus, speaking to the body—so cold in death, and all bound in grave clothes—said:

"Young man, I say unto thee, Arise."

What, bidding the dead come to life? Yes, and immediately the young man sat up and spoke to the mother and to Eliphaz and these straightway fell upon his neck and kissed him.

The multitudes that beheld this mighty work were astonished beyond measure, fear came upon them and they began to glorify God, some saying that "a great prophet is risen up among us." Others that "God hath visited his people." Bar-elah and Eliab were as much amazed as any of the others, for, although, they had seen many mighty things done by Jesus, they had not for a moment thought of His having power to raise the dead.

Bar-elah and Eliab had only a moment with Eliphaz and his resurrected friend. That moment though, spent in conversation with the one who even then had the grave-clothes about him, produced an impression upon the heart of each of our boys, never to be effaced. As Eliphaz parted with the boys, he called to Eliab:

"Come spend a few days with us in Nain."

"We'll see," answered both boys at the same

time.

"I rather think we had better go for a few days, Eliab," said Bar-elah after Eliphaz had left them. "We are out of food and are both in need of rest and I am somewhat foot-sore from walking so much. I'm not used to it, you know. Then too, I can't understand all this that we have seen and am somewhat curious to see this young man again."

Eliab was desirous of following Jesus, but being concerned deeply for Bar-elah and knowing well that his feet were troubling him greatly he readily agreed to Bar-elah's proposition. An hour later the two were seated with Eliphaz, talking over the wonderful events of the day.

That night Bar-elah's feet troubled him so that he could not sleep at all. Twice Eliab arose and attended to them for him. Towards morning Bar-elah awoke Eliab saying to him:

"Eliab, I'm sick." And he was sick, too. Eliab found him suffering greatly. The next day was a very hard one for poor Bar-elah. Eliab did not leave his bed-side at all during the day. The days that followed were anxious ones. It seemed at times that Bar-elah's sickness would become very serious.

One day when Bar-elah seemed to be suffering the most, he drew Eliab to him, saying as he did so:

"Oh! Eliab I wish Jesus could come and put hand upon me and cure me as he did with the many whom we saw healed."

"Yes Elah, my boy, I wish He was here," replied Eliab. This had been the longing of Eliab's heart from the first.

After quite a siege, during which Eliab kept close to his friend and ministered to him constantly, Bar-elah began to mend and was soon able to be out again.

During all of this time Jesus and His disciples had been very busy. After leaving Nain He went with the twelve through all the cities and villages of Galilee, preaching everywhere the gospel of the kingdom. And He did many wonderful things. One day one possessed of a devil, who was also dumb and blind, was brought to Him and He cast out the devil and healed the man of his blindness and dumbness.

CHAPTER VIII.

"ELIAB," said Bar-elah one day after he was well again and the two boys were alone for a moment, "I think we had better start out to-morrow to find Jesus of Nazareth. It has been quite a long time since we have seen him. I am feeling real strong again and I think we had better go, Eliphaz just told me that he heard that he was in the neighborhood of the Sea of Galilee—not far from Capernaum. Shall we go, Eliab?"

"Alright, Elah, I'm ready, if you feel well enough," was Eliab's response. And so the boys decided to start on the second day and travel slowly until they should again be with Jesus.

While they were on their journey Jesus was discoursing to the multitudes, in parables. He spoke to them a parable concerning a barren-fig tree to teach men that they ought to bear fruit. Then too He spoke the parable of the sower. He told them how the sower went forth to sow and in his sowing some of the seed "fell by the way side; some fell upon a rock; some fell among thorns; other fell on good ground."

His disciples asked Him to explain this parable to them and He did so, telling them that this parable taught the various ways in which men hear and receive the word.

Said He: "The seed is the word of God.

"Those by the way side are they that hear; then cometh the devil, and taketh away the word out of their hearts, lest they should believe and be saved.

"They on the rock are they, which, when they hear, receive the word with joy; and these have no root, which for a while believe, and in time of temptation fall away.

"And that which fell among thorns are they, which, when they have heard, go forth, and are choked with cares and riches and pleasures of this life, and bring no fruit to perfection.

"But that on the good ground are they, which in an honest and good heart, having heard the word, keep it, and bring forth fruit with patience."

Other parables followed. One of the tares. Another teaching men that the kingdom of heaven was like a mustard seed; small in its beginnings, but increasing and becoming a refuge for the weary. One teaching that the kingdom was like leaven; silent yet sure and powerful in its workings.

Seeing the great throng of people about Him, Jesus quietly withdrew to the other side of the lake but on the way a tempest was encountered. Jesus, weary of body, had fallen asleep in the boat. The storm grew more fierce until it seemed to the disciples who were in the boat, that they must perish. The boat filled with water. They awoke Jesus and rising in their midst He quietly said to the boisterous sea:

"Peace, be still," and immediately the storm ceased and all was quiet. Then were those in the boat filled with amazement because of His mighty power, because even the wind and waves obeyed Him.

Upon reaching the other side two possessed with demons met Him and He caused the evil spirits to come out of them and to pass into a herd of swine near at hand and these, numbering about two thousand, in their madness, straightway rushed headlong into the sea and were destroyed.

Great fear came upon the people of that region when they heard what Jesus had done and they besought Him to leave the country.

Jesus returned to Capernaum and was gladly received by the people for they had been looking anxiously for His return.

While there Jairus, one of the rulers of the Synagogue, and whose daughter was sick unto death, came to Jesus and besought Him to go to his house and lay His hand upon her that she might not die. Jesus went but before they reached the house word was brought to Jairus that his daughter was dead. Jesus did not stop, however. He went to the house and going to where the body lay He took the maid by the hand and immediately she arose.

While on the way to the house of Jairus another mighty work was wrought. The people were thronging about Jesus as He walked with His disciples and Jairus. In the crowd was a woman who for twelve years had been suffering with an issue of blood. She had spent all she had upon physicians but had obtained no relief whatever. She was in fact worse than ever. She had heard of Jesus and His many mighty cures.

She had great faith in Him and was anxious to have Him cure her. As she pushed her way through the crowd she said to herself:

"If I may but touch his garment, I shall be whole." Gradually she came nearer to the blessed Jesus and finally by reaching forth her hand she was able to touch the hem of his garment. She did so and immediately she was cured. Jesus turning said to her:

"Daughter, be of good comfort: thy faith hath made thee whole; go in peace."

As Jesus went from the home of Jairus He was met by two blind men who besought Him to have mercy on them. He simply touched their eyes and immediately they had their sight restored to them.

After this He went forth into all the cities and villages, preaching the gospel and healing the sick, and many believed on Him.

During this time Bar-elah and Eliab had been slowly travelling over the road from Nain to Capernaum. They went only a short distance each day as Bar-elah found he was not as strong as he had thought himself to be. They visited in the towns through which they passed

One evening as they were going along the street of the little village where they were to spend the night, they met a young man whom they recognized as an acquaintance from Capernaum. After their formal greetings Bar-elah said:

"Did you hear anything while at home of the whereabouts of Jesus of Nazareth?"

"Yes, he is now not far from Capernaum," answered the young man and then he told them of all the mighty works of Jesus in Galilee, to which we have referred.

"I myself saw many of these things," said the young man. "Demons were cast out; the sick were healed; the blind had their eyes opened; the dumb spoke."

That night the boys stayed at the home of an old friend of Bar-elah's father. After they had retired they lay for sometime, talking about the news they had heard concerning Jesus.

"Oh Elah, I'm so anxious to see that face again and be with Him again," said Eliab.

"So am I, Eliab," was the response.

During the next few days they made excellent progress and reached Capernaum one day just at the setting of the sun. They went at once to the home of the uncle where they had stayed before. Their first inquiry was as to where Jesus could be found.

"He is some place along the coast of the sea," said the uncle. "I think that if you take a boat and cross the sea in the morning you will find him there."

Next morning at the dawn of day the two boys were up and on their way. They found many people about and upon inquiry found that they were going along the shore around to the place where Jesus was. It was some distance and our boys had to go slowly on Bar-elah's account, and they did not get around the northern end of the sea until late in the day. Suddenly they came in sight of a very great multitude of people.

"Ah," said Eliab, "I guess we have found Him, Elah." And they had for Jesus sat in the midst of the multitude. The day was drawing to a close. Just as the boys arrived Jesus had told His disciples to make the multitude sit down in bands of fifty, upon the grass, and the disciples went forth at once into the multitude to carry out the Lord's command.

"What do you suppose this can mean Elah," asked Eliab.

"I'm sure I can't tell you, Eliab. I wish we had been a little sooner; but we'll soon see."

When the multitude, (which numbered about five thousand men besides the women and children), was seated, every eye was again fastened upon Jesus. A small basket was handed to Him. It contained five loaves of bread and two small fishes.

"Can it be Eliab, that He is going to feed this great multitude?" whispered Bar-elah as he leaned over to Eliab. "The day is far spent, this is a desert place and the people are undoubtedly very hungry and weary, but where can He get enough for this great crowd?"

But see, what is it the Christ does? Every eye is upon Him. Everything is perfectly silent. Taking the five barley loaves in His hand, and the two small fishes, He lifted His eyes to heaven and blessed the food and then began to break the loaves and fishes and as He did so the fragments multiplied as they passed through His divine hands until there was before Him a great heap of fragments both of bread and fish. He then gave these to His disciples commanding them to distribute to the multitude. They did so and the entire multitude ate and was satisfied. Bar-elah and Eliab both ate of the bread and fish and as they did so looked at one another in astonishment.

"What wonderful thing will He do next Elah?" asked Eliab in his amazement.

Bar-elah only shook his head. He was as much astonished as was Eliab. After the multitude had been fully satisfied, it was seen that a large pile of fragments remained.

"Gather up the fragments that remain," commanded Jesus of his disciples, "that nothing be lost," and they filled twelve baskets with the fragments that remained.

"How strange," thought Bar-elah," that One who can produce bread at his will, would bother to save the fragments." But this was another evidence of His greatness, for He wastes nothing.

Jesus directed His disciples to take a boat and cross the sea to Bethsaida while He dismissed the multitude. Slowly the throng dispersed and Jesus withdrew to a quiet place to pray. Bar-elah and Eliab went back to Capernaum to spend a few days. Before the disciples had reached the other side, they saw a new evidence of His power. The little boat in which the disciples were, was tossed about furiously by the wind that had arisen. Suddenly they saw one approaching them, walking upon the water. They were troubled, thinking it to be a spirit, but all fears subsided when they heard the familiar voice of Jesus saying to them:

"It is I; be not afraid."

In Gennesaret He healed many sick, and preached the gospel to the multitudes that thronged about Him.

The next day, the multitude that had been fed, took shipping to Capernaum. They found Jesus there in the Synagogue and began at once to question Him. Our two young men were near at hand and heard all that was said.

"Ye seek me, not because ye saw the miracles, but because ye did eat of the loaves, and were filled," said Jesus to the multitude. "Labor not for the meat which perisheth, but for that meat which endureth unto everlasting life, which the Son of man shall give unto you."

Other very blessed and gracious words fell from his lips. Said he;

"My Father **giveth you** the true bread from heaven. For the **bread of God** is he which cometh down from heaven, and giveth life **unto the** world. * * I am the bread of life. * * This is the **bread** which cometh down from heaven, that a **man** may eat thereof, and not die."

These words and the many others **He spoke,** astonished the multitude. **They could not understand** how they **could eat of** the bread of which **He** spoke. Eliab though felt that he could understand the Christ, at least to **some extent,** for he realized that his own soul had been satisfied by **this One** who called Himself "the bread of life."

CHAPTER IX.

THE time for the Feast of Tabernacles drew near. Again every road leading to Jerusalem was crowded with pilgrims. Jesus and His disciples were among those who went up to the Feast. Bar-elah and Eliab also.

Six months had passed since the discourse at Capernaum, when Jesus announced Himself as the Bread of Life. During that time He with His disciples, and followed by a great multitude of people, Bar-elah and Eliab being in the throng,—He with these had journeyed through the region about Tyre and Sidon, Cæsarea Philippi, through Galilee and Samaria.

Near Tyre and Sidon He had healed the daughter of a Syrophœnician woman. This one had been tormented with a devil. The mother had come to Jesus for help, beseeching Him to heal her daughter. When Jesus saw her faith He said unto her: "O woman, great is thy faith; be it unto thee even as thou wilt," and forthwith her daughter was healed.

Near the Sea of Galilee, Jesus went up into a mountain. Many who were sick were brought unto Him and He healed them. The multitude numbered four thousand men besides women and children. These Jesus fed as He had previously fed the five thousand, producing food miraculously for them.

At Bethsaida Jesus healed one who had been blind.

While in the region of Cæsarea Philippi, Jesus in speaking to His disciples told them of His approaching death and resurrection. He told them He must needs go up to Jerasulem and there suffer many things and be put to death—but after that He would rise again. These are the words He had used:

"The Son of man must suffer many things, and be rejected of the elders and chief priests and scribes, and be slain, and be raised the third day."

Some eight days after this Jesus took some of His disciples up into a mountain, to pray. While praying He was transfigured before them, His ountenance shone and His raiment was changed until it too, seemed to shine. While thus transfigured two, having the appearance of Moses and Elias, talked with Him.

While at Capernaum Jesus miraculously provided the tribute money needed by Himself and Peter. He directed Peter to go to the sea and there he was to take the first fish caught and in its mouth would be found the money. Peter did as commanded and found all as Jesus had said.

From Capernaum Jesus sent out seventy disciples to do work for Him. These He first fully instructed as to what they should do and say. To them He gave the power to heal the sick and to cast out devils.

After these things He departed from Galilee to go up to Jerusalem to attend the Feast of Tabernacles. As He went through Samaria, when He came to a certain village, ten lepers came to him. They did not come near to Him as did some of the others whom He cleansed, but stood at a distance and cried with a loud voice: "Jesus, Master, have mercy on us." One of the men was a Samaritan, would Jesus cleanse him, too? He was one of those who had cried out for mercy. Oh! what a pitiful sight they were as they stood afar off, afraid to come near lest they might defile the Christ! Afraid to approach any man, constantly crying out, "Unclean, unclean," as they went about, to warn the people that they might not come near them. This is the question Bar-elah and Eliab were asking themselves. Listen; it is Jesus who speaks:

"Go show yourselves unto the priests." And they went and were cleansed. But one of them returns. He is the Samaritan. What is it he wants? He is heard to speak—he is giving glory to God for his being healed. He approaches Jesus, falls prostrate at His feet, pouring forth his thanks as he does so. "Were there not ten cleansed?" Asked Jesus. "But where are the nine? There are not found that returned to give glory to God, save this stranger,"—he being a Samaritan, "Arise, go thy way; thy faith hath made thee whole."

Those who saw it marvelled. Jesus sought to go privately to Jerusalem and but a small number were now with Him. Bar-elah and Eliab had both managed to keep near Him and were, in fact, able at times to come closer to Him for the people did not throng Him as before. The nearer they came the greater the influences they felt, from His divine, His sacred person.

They draw nigh to Jerusalem. In the distance they could see the walls of the Holy City.

"We shall soon be there Elah," said Eliab.

"Oh! Eliab, I feel as though I cannot take another step! I am feeling so sick again and my feet are so sore." And poor Bar-elah did look about worn out. Eliab had noticed this in his friend but thought it was from the excitement and that when they reached Jerusalem he would be alright.

"I must stop here Eliab and lie down. Oh! I'm so sick," and Bar-elah fell in a faint. Eliab soon brought him to. He spread his cloak out for him and laid him on it.

"Shall I call Jesus, Elah?" asked Eliab,

"Yes," gasped Bar-elah. When the Christ came, seeing Eliab's faith, He put forth His hand and touched Bar-elah and immediately he was made well and arose.

"Oh! that that sacred touch would awaken a response in my boy's heart," said Eliab within himself. Bar-elah did look thoughtful.

"Oh! Eliab, I'm so full of iniquity, it hardly

seems right to have allowed the Christ to have put his holy hand upon me for fear of his becoming defiled."

"Let Him cleanse your soul my boy. Ask Him to speak the word of forgiveness," said Eliab. Bar-elah said nothing.

Jerusalem looked bright and full of life. The City was crowded. Long before the boys had reached the city gate they began to meet acquaintances among the crowds they met. In some way they lost track of Jesus.

The streets of the City were lined with booths made of the branches of trees. In the temple court these booths were to be seen. On the roofs of the houses, also. In these the people lived during the feast. This festival was kept to commemorate the forty years wanderings of their forefathers in the wilderness before entering into Canaan. It was also kept as a season of thanksgiving for the ingathering of the harvest.

The City presented a very beautiful appearance with its many booths. Bar-elah and Eliab found the people happy and gay all of them busy getting ready for the first day of the feast which was a Sabbath to the Lord. The boys went at once to the home where they had, with their families, celebrated the Passover. There they found both families again enjoying the hospitality of Eliab's uncle.

That evening the two boys were kept busy relating their wonderful experiences while following Jesus from place to place. Eliab's mother knew before of her boy's faith in this One and his joy in believing and now that he was with her she could see that he had, indeed, experienced rich things.

"And you really believe, Eliab, that this One is the long-looked-for Messiah of the Jews?" she asked.

"I know it, mother."

CHAPTER X.

IN Jerusalem the people sought for Jesus and found Him in the temple, where He taught them. They were all astonished at His teaching and learning. His doctrines were so different from many of theirs.

Evidently there was some plot to put Jesus to death, for Bar-elah was astonished beyond measure by overhearing one say to another:

"Is not this he, whom they seek to kill?"

"What," said Bar-elah when he had communicated this to Eliab, "seeking to kill the one who has healed me? Not if I can prevent it." Both boys felt almost terrified for the time, for even then the chief priests and the Pharisees sought to take Him.

·

The close of the feast drew nigh. All were looking forward to the last day, which was the great day of all. Everybody seemed to have had a blessed time but looked to this great day as being the best.

The day dawned. Our two young men were out early. The streets of the Holy City were alive with people. Bar-elah and Eliab were going towards the temple. It was a warm day and the multitudes were very thirsty. Suddenly a voice was heard above the noise made by the crowd, Bar-elah heard it and these are the words he heard:

"If any man thirst, let him come unto me and drink."

"Oh," said Bar-elah to Eliab, "only some one trying to call attention to his wares"—and yet that thought did not stay with him long when he remembered the day, it being a sacred day, and also the place. The next words he heard told him he was mistaken:

"He that believeth on me, as the Scripture hath said, out of his belly shall flow rivers of living water."

"What strange doctrine is this Elah?" asked Eliab as the two boys gently pushed their way through the crowd with the hope of being able to see the one whose voice they had heard.

"Why Eliab," said Bar-elah when he caught sight of the face—"it is Jesus."

The feast was over. Slowly the crowds dispersed as the people wended their ways homeward.

The next day, in the temple, one who had been a great sinner, was brought to Jesus. This one was brought by the Scribes and Pharisees, for they had hoped to lay a snare for the Christ, that they might catch Him and put Him to death. Jesus knew their hearts and thoughts. The Pharisees and Scribes questioned Him, tempting Him. Looking upon them and then upon the woman He said:

"He that is without sin among you, let him first cast a stone at her," for they had asked Him if she ought be stoned to death because of her sin. They answered Him not a word. Nor did any cast a stone, but quietly, one by one they went out, realizing that a beam was in their own eyes as well as the woman's. Their consciences convicted them. When they had all gone out Jesus forgave the woman of her great sin and bid her "go, and sin no more." When the people came together about Him again He said to them:

"I am the light of the world: he that followeth me shall not walk in darkness, but shall have the light of life.

"Ye are from beneath; I am from above: ye are of this world; I am not of this world. I said therefore unto you, that ye shall die in your sins; for if ye believe not that I am he, ye shall die in your sins."

And many other things did He speak unto them as He taught in the temple, and many of the Jews believed on Him because of these sayings.

To those who believed He said:

"If ye continue in my word, then are ye my disciples indeed; and ye shall know the truth, and the truth shall make you free."

And to those Jews who sought to destroy Him, He said:

"But now ye seek to kill me, a man that hath told you the truth, which I have heard of God."

Bar-elah and Eliab looked at one another in wonder.

"Surely," said Eliab, "He must know of all their plans."

"If a man keep my saying," continued Jesus, "he shall never see death."

Upon hearing this the Jews charged Him with having a devil, because, said they, Abraham and the prophets all saw death. These Jews became indignant and full of wrath and took up stones to hurl at Him. Bar-elah quickly grasped the arm of one who stood next him, in whose hand was a stone ready to be thrown.

"He speaks the truth," said Bar-elah.

Quietly Jesus withdrew Himself from the temple, passing through the midst of the excited Jews.

A little later Jesus spoke the parable of the good Samaritan, telling how a certain man fell among thieves who used him shamefully and then left him, torn and bleeding and wounded, by the wayside. A priest happened by but would not help the suffering one. Then a Levite came along, and he too, neglected to aid the wounded man; but finally a poor, despised, hated Samaritan came along and his heart was filled with pity and he straightway dressed his wounds and put him upon his beast and cared for him. Jesus spoke this parable to teach a certain lawyer who had temptingly asked Him certain questions, who his neighbor was for this one had said to Jesus:

"And who is my neighbor?"

After this Jesus went to Bethany where He abode a short time. That night Bar-elah and Eliab remained in Jerusalem still enjoying the hospitality of the uncle.

"Elah," said Eliab after they had finished the evening meal, "suppose we abide here a few days. I desire to learn something more if I can about the plot these priests and scribes have in mind, whereby they hope to destroy Jesus."

"Alright, Eliab," said Bar-elah.

On the morning they set out to learn what they could. As they walked along the street they saw quite a crowd upon one of the corners. They recognized several as being scribes and Pharisees. They drew near and found they were discussing the Christ.

"This man makes himself equal with God. He blasphemes. He is worthy of death," said one excited scribe.

"He is turning the heads of the people," said another.

"His doctrine is dangerous to our law," said

a self-righteous, pompous looking old **Pharisee.**

And these and the other accusations brought, **they** considered **as sufficient** to warrant His **being** put to death.

Bar-elah and **Eliab were silent.** They **knew not whether to** speak **or keep silence.** As **they left the** crowd, **Bar-elah** spoke:

"**Oh!** Eliab, **what can** we do**! It seems an** outrage that these hard-hearted **Jews should be** plotting against this One who seems **so pure and who has done** such wondrous **things. What can we do?**"

"**I'm sure I** don't know, Elah. **But see how He passed** through the midst **of them when they sought** to stone Him and **how He** has escaped out of their hands. Perhaps it would be so when they seek to kill Him, Elah."

CHAPTER XI.

JESUS had returned to Jerusalem. The seventy whom He had sent out two by two had returned. One who had been born blind had been healed so that he saw as perfectly as any one. Jesus had said in answer to a question from His disciples; asked before He had healed the man:

"Neither hath this man sinned, nor his parents; but that the works of God should be made manifest in him."

When Jesus had made an ointment of clay and spittle and put it upon his eyes, He bade the man go wash in Siloam. He did as commanded and at once could see. This was done on the Sabbath and the Pharisees thought they had another crime to charge against Jesus.

After this, in His discourse, Jesus said:

"Verily, verily, I say unto you, He that entereth not by the door into the sheepfold, but climbeth up some other way, the same is a thief and a robber. But he that entereth in by the door is the shepherd of the sheep. To him the porter openeth; and the sheep hear his voice; and he calleth his own sheep by name, and leadeth them out. And when he putteth forth his own sheep, he goeth before them, and the sheep follow him: for they know his voice. And a stranger will they not follow, but will flee from him; for they know not the voice of strangers."

"Verily, verily, I say unto you, I am the door of the sheep. All that ever came before me are thieves and robbers: but the sheep did not hear them. I am the door: by me if any man enter in, he shall be saved, and shall go in and out, and find pasture. The thief cometh not, but for to steal, and to kill, and destroy: I am come that they might have life, and that they might have it more abundantly. I am the good shepherd; the good shepherd giveth his life for the sheep."

Bar-elah and Eliab, heard these words. Eliab understood them but Bar-elah did not. As they went forth from the presence of Jesus, they saw Eliphaz who had come from Capernaum to be present at Jerusalem at the feast of dedication.

"O, Eliphaz," called Bar-elah when he and Eliab got within speaking distance. Eliphaz knew the voice and turned. His face was radiant. To Bar-elah it was more attractive than ever. His countenance spoke of joy within.

"I've entered through the door into the fold, friend Eliab," were the first words Eliphaz spoke.

"Give God the glory," was Eliab's response. Bar-elah silently grasped the hand of Eliphaz. "You must come and abide with us Eliphaz," said Eliab. He gladly went with them. Upon the house-top that night they had a long and earnest talk—Eliab and Eliphaz telling of the wondrous joy that they had found. Bar-elah was deeply impressed with what he heard from the boys and found himself longing for the same experiences of joy and peace, they seemed to have.

The Feast of Dedication was a time of great rejoicing, commemorating the re-dedication of the sacred temple, after its terrible defilement by the wicked Antiochus Epiphanes.

Jesus and His disciples attended the festival. One day the Jews after asking Him questions, took up stones ready to stone Him to death; but He escaped from them and went to Bethany, beyond Jordan, where He abode.

Bar-elah, Eliab and Eliphaz heard that He was there and forthwith, they too, went to Bethany.

In this town one named Lazarus lay sick. This one was loved by Jesus. The sisters of this man, Mary and Martha, sent to Jesus, saying:

"Lord, behold, he whom thou **lovest** is sick."

They thought He would straightway come and heal their brother but He abode where He was two days, and then returned to Judæa. After this He said to His disciples:

"Our friend Lazarus sleepeth ; but I go, that I may awake him out of sleep."

So Jesus went, and His disciples with Him. Bar-elah, Eliab and Eliphaz were still in Bethany having remained there when Jesus went into Judæa. As Jesus and His disciples drew nigh unto Bethany Martha the sister of Lazarus went forth to meet Him. When she met Him she said:

"Lord, if thou hadst been here, my brother had not died. But I know, that even now, whatsoever thou wilt ask of God, God will give it thee."

Jesus answered her saying:

"Thy brother shall rise again."

" I know that he shall rise again," said Martha, "in the resurrection at the last day."

"I," answered Jesus, "am the resurrection and the life: he that believeth in me, though he were dead, yet shall he live; and whosoever liveth and believeth in me shall never die."

Soon after Mary heard from Martha, who had returned to the house, that Jesus was coming and so she went out to meet Him. Many Jews also followed thinking she was going to the tomb to weep. Bar-elah, Eliab and Eliphaz met the little company and joined them, not knowing what it all meant. Soon the boys saw Jesus approaching and their hearts bounded with delight.

"I'm glad," said Eliab, "that this poor woman is going to Jesus with her sorrow."

Mary, when she met Jesus, fell at His feet, weeping and saying as Martha had before:

"Lord, if thou hadst been here, my brother had not died."

The whole company went to the cave in which the body of Lazarus had lain for four days.

Jesus said:

"Take ye away the stone," and when they had done so, Jesus cried aloud saying:

"Lazarus, come forth," and straightway he

came forth.

"Eliphaz," said Bar-elah who with his two companions had witnessed it all, "this is more wonderful than the raising of your friend, for this one had been dead four days. Surely this Jesus must be of God. No man could do such wonderful things if God were not with him."

How the hearts of these three young men would have ached had they known that some Jews, who witnessed this miracle, at once went to the Pharisees and told them all about it, and that these Pharisees and the chief priests at once counseled together as to how they might put Jesus to death!

Bar-elah and Eliab remained in Bethany some days and later spent some time in their own village, while Jesus and His disciples went into Ephraim and into Peræa.

Great multitudes followed the Christ into the country beyond Jordan. While there in Peræa one Sabbath He healed a woman who for eighteen years had suffered greatly and was bent together so that she could not stand upright.

Again Jesus set His face towards Jerusalem. And as He went He taught the people. Many were the parables He uttered. There was the one of the lost sheep, speaking of the efforts made to reclaim any that may be lost, and the joy when the lost is found, and ending with these words:

"I say unto you, that likewise joy shall be in heaven over one sinner that repenteth, more than over ninety and nine just persons, which need no repentance."

Then there was the parable of the lost pieces of silver, teaching the same truth. Then He spoke the parable of the prodigal son, telling how a young man left his father's house, and went into a distant country where he squandered what he had and then in his poverty and need became a swine-herd, a task most degrading to a Jew. The poor young man was in great need and sought to satisfy his hunger on the husks thrown out for the swine. Finally he thought on his ways, repented of his sin and set his face towards his father's house. There he was received with a royal welcome. This parable was to teach men the course of the sinner and the welcome and forgiveness awaiting him in the Father's house.

There was the parable of the unjust steward, followed by the words:

"No servant can serve two masters: for either he will hate the one, and love the other; or else he will hold to the one, and despise the other. Ye cannot serve God and mammon."

Then He spake the parable of the rich man and Lazarus, telling of the suffering in hell of the one who was sinful, and the joy and felicity of the other among the redeemed. Many other teachings followed. Large numbers of children were brought to Him and upon these He put His hands and blessed them. It was a beautiful sight to behold. There sat the Great Teacher, surrounded by those who had brought the children to Him. One by one He would take these precious little ones up into His arms and breathe a blessing upon them.

"How tender and loving," said Eliab to Bareliah, as they saw the Christ do this.

As Jesus and His disciples, Bar-elah and Eliab, among them, went forth, they saw one approaching in the distance. He seemed to be in very great haste as he was running. As he drew near it was seen that he was a young man, and a ruler. When he reached Jesus he threw himself on the ground before Him, beseeching Him to tell him what he must do to have eternal life. Jesus told him to keep the commandments. These, he said, he had kept from his youth up, but realizing that this was not sufficient and that there was more for him to do he asked Jesus this question, "what lack I yet?" and Jesus seeing the lack and that the young man, who was rich, was to some extent selfish, He said to him:

"Go and sell that thou hast, and give to the poor, and thou shalt have treasure in heaven: and come and follow me."

But the young man turned away grieved, prefering to keep his great riches for his own use, than do as Jesus directed and thus obtain eternal life.

Jesus continued to speak to the people in parables. On the way up to Jerusalem He again foretold His death and resurrection, to His twelve disciples, saying to them:

"Behold, we go up to Jerusalem; and the Son of man shall be betrayed unto the chief priests and unto the scribes, and they shall condemn him to death, and shall deliver him to the Gentiles to mock, and to scourge, and to crucify him: and the third day he shall rise again."

Bar-elah had had word from his father which made it necessary for him to go to his home at once. He did so, accompanied by Eliab. The business matter was soon settled.

"Elah, I just heard on the street that Jesus is on His way to Jerusalem and if we hurry we will be in time to meet Him in Jericho," said Eliab to his friend.

"Alright, Eliab, let us haste to Jericho."

They at once set out and reached the city just as Jesus and His disciples, followed by a very great multitude, were leaving. The two young men went with them. As they left the city they saw old blind Bartimæus sitting by the wayside begging. This one when he heard that Jesus was passing cried out to Him for mercy and the Christ opened his eyes.

While in Jericho, as Jesus and the multitude that pressed about Him, were passing along the street of the city, Jesus looked up into a sycamore tree growing along side the road and there saw one named Zacchæus, a rich man, one of the chief publicans, who, because of his smallness of stature, had climbed into the tree that he might see Jesus. As Jesus passed He called to Zacchæus, saying that He desired to abide at his house. Zacchæus received his divine guest gladly, and received salvation.

Before going to Jerusalem, Jesus spent a little time in the home of Lazarus. Bar-elah and Eliab went on to Jerusalem. There the people were busy preparing for the passover, for there were but six days remaining before the feast.

Just as Eliab had finished his evening meal, Bar-elah came into the room all excitement.

"Eliab," said he, "come up stairs I want to tell you something."

They went up to the house-top. Eliab wondered what was troubling his companion.

"Could you believe it Eliab," said Bar-elah as soon as they were alone, "those Pharisees and chief priests are planning to take Jesus as soon as he enters the city, and put him to death! I just discovered the plot. It is quite well known among the scribes and I overheard them counselling together. They didn't know I was around. What can we do Eliab?"

"My dear Elah, I've no idea what to do," said Eliab.

"He ought not to die, Eliab," was Bar-elah's response.

CHAPTER XII.

Upon the first day of the week, Bar-elah and Eliab arose early and, after the morning meal, went to the temple. They remained there but a short time and then walked about the city some. As they slowly walked along they were met by quite a multitude of people, some of them carrying branches of palms. The throng was hastening towards the gate of the City.

"What can this mean, Elah?" asked Eliab.

"I'm sure I can't imagine Eliab, let us follow them and see," answered Bar-elah.

And so the two young men joined the throng. Bar-elah walked alongside of a young man of his own age.

"Where is this multitude going and what mean the palm branches?" asked Bar-elah of this one.

"We are going forth from the City to meet Jesus of Nazareth, the Christ of God," was the young man's reply. "He is approaching the City. We have heard His wonderful teachings and seen His mighty works, and believe Him to be the Messias."

Bar-elah looked at Eliab. The latter said:

"Yes, and I too, believe in Him."

The multitude went forth from the City. In a short time a multitude was seen approaching them. In the lead was one sitting upon the colt of an ass. When they drew nearer Eliab was quick to recognize the One who rode, as Jesus the Christ.

"There He is Elah, riding upon the ass," said Eliab. Elah looked.

"Yes, Eliab, that is he." The multitudes met. There was great rejoicing. The whole company, waiving the branches of palms, began to praise and to glorify God, saying:

"Hosanna to the son of David: Blessed is he that cometh in the name of the Lord; Hosanna in the highest."

Many spread their garments before the Christ that He might ride over them. Others of the great multitude scattered palm branches in the way. One multitude went before Him and one behind Him. They followed Him into the city waving their palm branches and singing their hosannas to God. There was great rejoicing. Our two young men mingled their voices with the rest. Eliab sang with all his heart and he noticed that his Elah sang as heartily as any. Before they entered the City, however, when they came near it, Jesus wept over it because of the unbelief of the people and that which would come upon the City in time to come.

As the demonstrative multitude entered the Holy City, the people of the City were filled with wonder and many asked:

"Who is this?"

Those in the multitude answered, saying:

"This is Jesus the prophet of Nazareth of Galilee."

All this only vexed the unbelieving Pharisees the more. They were filled with wrath, saying among themselves:

"Perceive ye how ye prevail nothing? behold, the world is gone after him." They were the more determined to kill Him. That night He went, with the twelve, to Bethany and abode there. On the morrow He returned to Jerusalem and went at once to the temple. There He found those that bought and sold and thus made the place an house of merchandise. These He cast out, saying as He did so:

"It is written, My house shall be called the house of prayer; but ye have made it a den of thieves."

Many who were sick and lame and blind came to Him in the temple and He healed them all. This was on the second day of the week. Towards even Jesus and the twelve went again to Bethany.

The next morning, Bar-elah and Eliab, before they arose, began to discuss their plans for the day.

"I think Elah," said Eliab, "that we had better watch at the City gate for Jesus, when He shall return from Bethany, and then keep close to Him all the day. He probably will spend much time in the temple."

"That would be a good plan Eliab," said Bar-elah.

"My dear Elah," said Eliab after a little, as he drew his friend to him, "will you not accept Jesus as your own Lord and Master that you too, may be His?"

"Eliab," said Bar-elah in response as he slipped his arm about the one the power and influences of whose love he had long felt, and whom he acknowledged to be his best friend, "I know I am not what I ought to be, but, Eliab, I mean from this time forth to leave off some of my bad habits. You know what they are. I mean to live a different life from what I heretofore have lived. Truly, Eliab, since you and I have been following this Jesus around, my conscience has been troubling me. He is so pure that one, who is impure, cannot help but feel his own wickedness. I have felt it my friend, and I mean to do better and I know you'll help me to."

"Indeed, I will Elah and may God grant you His favor and help," said Eliab out of a full heart.

An hour later the two boys were standing together at the City gate waiting for the coming of Jesus. He soon arrived accompanied by His disciples. The boys joined them. They all went at once into the temple. There He taught the people, many of His teachings being in the form of parables.

One parable that impressed Eliab forcibly was the one telling of the husbandmen to whom a vineyard was let. To these the householder sent, at the proper season, to receive of the fruit, but the husbandmen shamefully used the servants who had been sent, even killing one of them. The second company sent was treated likewise. Finally the householder sent his own beloved son thinking they dare not use him despitefully, but the husbandmen slew him also. When Jesus had explained the parable the chief priests and Pharisees saw clearly, that He referred to them. They became so angry that they sought to lay violent hands on Him, but they feared those who believed on Him.

The parable of the marriage of the king's son, followed. The Sadducees sought to tempt Him with questions about tribute to Cæsar and about the resurrection, but He soon put them to silence, so that they dared not ask Him another question. Then the Pharisees came forward to ensnare him. One of them, a lawyer, asked Him about the commandments—as to which was greatest. Jesus answered, "Thou shalt love the Lord thy God with all thy heart, and with all thy soul, and with all thy mind. This is the first and great commandment. And the second is like unto it, Thou shalt love thy neighbour as thyself. On these two commandments hang all the law and the prophets." Then Jesus put to them this question?

"What think ye of Christ? whose son is he?" And in their answering Jesus silenced them so they too, dared ask Him no more questions.

It did Bar-elah lots of good to see these self-important, conceited, self-righteous Pharisees put to silence.

"Didn't he shut that old fellow up in a hurry though," he whispered to Eliab, as his handsome face beamed with delight.

Jesus was so fearless in his denunciation of the scribes and Pharisees, that all about were amazed. Said He:

"But woe unto you, scribes and Pharisees, hypocrites! for ye shut up the kingdom of heaven against men: for ye neither go in yourselves, neither suffer ye them that are entering to go in. Woe unto you, scribes and Pharisees, hypocrites! for ye devour widows' houses, and for a pretence make long prayer: therefore ye shall receive the greater damnation.

"Woe unto you, scribes and Pharisees, hypocrites! for ye make clean the outside of the cup and of the platter, but within they are full of extortion and excess.

"Thou blind Pharisee, cleanse first that which is within the cup and platter, that the outside of them may be clean also.

"Woe unto you, scribes and Pharisees, hypocrites! for ye are like unto whited sepulchres, which indeed appear beautiful outward, but are within full of dead men's bones, and of all uncleanness.

"Even so ye also outwardly appear righteous unto men, but within ye are full of hypocrisy and iniquity." And this He said before all the people. Many other woes were pronounced against them because of their iniquities.

While He was teaching a party of Greeks who had come to attend the passover, came to Philip saying:

"Sir, we would see Jesus." Andrew and Philip went and told Jesus. While Jesus was talking to them a voice from heaven spoke to Him. Some of those who heard it thought it was thunder while Bar-elah and Eliab and many others thought an angel spoke with Jesus. It filled all with wonder.

As Jesus and His disciples went forth from the temple He told them of its destruction, when, as He said:

"There shall not be left here one stone upon another, that shall not be thrown down."

He also told of the persecution they, as His disciples, should suffer. He spoke the parable of the ten virgins to teach the disciples the necessity of their watching constantly for the coming of the hour in which "the Son of man," (meaning Himself), should return.

Then He spoke the parable of the talents to teach the duty of each one using the talents, the powers, the opportunities given by God.

Before leaving the Mount of Olives, to which He and His disciples had gone after leaving the temple, Jesus described to them the last judgment, when, as He said:

"The Son of man shall come in his glory, and all the holy angels with him, then shall he sit upon the throne of his glory: and before him shall be gathered all nations: and he shall separate them one from another, as a shepherd divideth his sheep from the goats: and he shall set the sheep on his right hand, but the goats on the left.

"Then shall the King say unto them on his right hand, Come, ye blessed of my Father, inherit the kingdom prepared for you from the foundation of the world. * * "Then shall he say also unto them on the left hand, Depart from me, ye cursed, into everlasting fire, prepared for the devil and his angels: * * and these shall go away into everlasting punishment: but the righteous into life eternal."

Immediately after this the chief priests and scribes and elders gathered together in the palace of Caiaphas the high priest, that they might plot to take Jesus and kill him. One of the twelve whom Jesus had chosen, one named Judas Iscariot, the one who had acted as treasurer of the little band, one who had seen the mighty works which Jesus had done and had attended upon His ministry, but who loved money more than the Lord, went to these chief priests and others and said to them:

"What will ye give me, and I will deliver him unto you?"

"Thirty pieces of silver," said they. Judas agreed.

CHAPTER XIII.

THE disciples of the Lord had prepared the passover, and when evening had come, they sat down to the passover meal. After supper Jesus greatly astonished His disciples for, after He had girded Himself with a towel, He filled a basin with water and then washed the feet of each disciple. How strange! What an example of humility! The Son of God taking upon Himself the work of the lowliest servant! The disciples were deeply impressed.

While they sat at meat, the disciples were greatly surprised and saddened to have Jesus say to them:

"One of you shall betray me." Each began to ask:

"Is it I?" John, the one whom Jesus loved so dearly, and who reclined on Jesus' bosom at the supper, asked:

"Lord, who is it?"

"He it is, to whom I shall give a sop, when I have dipped it," said Jesus. When the sop was dipped it was handed to Judas Iscariot, and he at once went out.

Jesus spent some little time talking with His disciples. He knew the hour in which Judas should betray Him and He should be put to death, was drawing near. He had much to say to His little band. He told them what things should happen to them. He told how Simon Peter should deny Him. He comforted them with many blessed assurances and promises.

After He had prayed with His disciples, they went out to Gethsemane. Jesus took Peter, James and John with Him, apart from the others, and bade them watch there with Him. He went a short distance from these. They could hear Him praying. He seemed to be in very great agony. His prayer was:

"O my Father, if it be possible, let this cup pass from me: nevertheless not as I will, but as thou wilt." The agony He suffered was intense. So great was it, because of the burden of His soul, that He sweat great drops of blood.

When He returned to His disciples He found them asleep. He awakened them and said:

"Rise up, let us go; lo, he that betrayeth me is at hand."

As they went they were met by Judas Iscariot, who was accompanied by a band of officers, and a very great multitude and into the hands of these, the traitor betrayed the Christ, by a kiss, for he had said to them: "Whomsoever I shall kiss, that same is he: hold him fast."

The officers at once laid hands on Jesus. He offered no resistance for He knew that His hour had come. Peter, however, drew a sword and cut off the ear of the high priest's servant, but Jesus rebuked him and touched the ear and healed it.

To those who came out against Him, He said:

"Are ye come out, as against a thief, with swords and with staves to take me? I was daily with you in the temple teaching, and ye took me not."

They bound Him and led Him——the Christ, the Messiah, the Lord, the Holy One of God—— led Him away——a prisoner.

He was at once taken before Caiaphas the high priest, before whom all the chief priests, scribes and elders had gathered. Peter, one of the twelve, followed Jesus at a distance but would not go further than the servant's hall. There he sat and warmed himself before the fire, while his Master was being shamefully maltreated within. While there in the midst of the servants of the high priest, three times Peter wickedly denied all acquaintance with Jesus. He even sought to affirm his wicked denial with an oath. Just as he had uttered the third denial he heard the cock crow. Peter was now where he could see Jesus as he stood in the palace of Caiaphas. Just as Peter had uttered his third denial, Jesus turned toward him. The guilty disciple saw the look of his divine Master and that look nearly broke his sinful heart for at once he remembered what Jesus had said to him:—

"Before the cock crow, thou shalt deny me thrice."

Peter was exceedingly sorrowful and went out and wept bitter tears of repentance.

During this time Jesus was being examined by Caiaphas, who questioned Him first, as to the disciples He had made and then as to the doctrine He had taught. The council produced false witnesses against Him, hoping by means of these to secure His condemnation and death. But even these did not answer the purpose intended.

One witness testified:

"This fellow said, 'I am able to destroy the temple of God, and to build it in three days.'" When Jesus did not answer to this, but kept silence, the high priest arose and demanded that He tell them whether or not He was the Christ, the Son of God.

Jesus answered: "Thou hast said: nevertheless I say unto you, Hereafter shall ye see the Son of man sitting on the right hand of power, and coming in the clouds of heaven."

This angered Caiaphas and in his wrath he arose, and rent his clothes, and said:

"He hath spoken blasphemy; what further need have we of witnesses? behold, now ye have heard his blasphemy. What think ye?" To this the scribes, the elders and the chief priests answered:

"He is guilty of death."

Then they all began to mock Him and to use Him most shamefully.

Oh! how the hearts of Bar-elah and Eliab would have ached had they been able just then to see this One whom they had followed and whom Eliab loved so! If they could have had one glimpse at the face, to them so full of love and beauty, as one after another of the wicked council smote Him in the face with their hands, and some of them even went so far as to spit in His face! Oh, to what depths of iniquity will man sink!

They bound Him and when it was day, they led Him before Pontius Pilate the Governor of Judæa. The Jews would not enter the Judgment Hall, lest they might become defiled and not be able to eat the passover. Surely was not this doing as Jesus had told the Pharisees they did—when He said: "ye blind guides, which strain at a gnat and swallow a camel."

Pilate questioned Jesus carefully regarding the matters charged against Him by the Jews, and finding no charge that could be sustained against Him, he went out to where the Jews were and said to them:

"I find no fault in this man."

When Pilate found that Jesus was from Galilee he at once sent Him to Herod, the tetrarch of that province, who happened to be in Jerusalem just then.

Herod was very glad to see Jesus for he had heard of the many great and wonderful things He had done, but had never before seen Him. He too examined Jesus but found no fault in Him. So after he and his soldiers had mocked Him, he sent Him back to Pilate.

Pilate called the chief priests, and elders and scribes together and said to them: "Ye have brought this man unto me, as one that perverteth the people; and, behold, I, having examined him before you, have found no fault in this man touching those things whereof ye accuse him: No, nor yet Herod: for I sent you to him; and, lo, nothing worthy of death is done unto him. I will therefore chastise him, and release him."

For it was customary at this feast of the passover, to release unto the Jews, one prisoner and Pilate remembered that he held as prisoner one Barabbas, a desperate fellow, and he thought he would give the Jews their choice between Barabbas and Jesus, expecting them to choose Jesus in preference to wicked Barabbas who had given them so much trouble, while it was known by all that Jesus had done many great things for the people, and Pilate was really anxious to release Him.

Pilate therefore, went forth to the Jews and suggested that he release Jesus but to his great amazement the Jews, incited by the chief priests, demanded Barabbas, and when Pilate asked what he should do with Jesus, they all began to cry out:

"Let him be crucified."

Pilate tried to reason with them, but all in vain for the Jews only cried out the louder:

"Crucify him, crucify him."

So Pilate released Barabbas and took Jesus and scourged Him and then delivered Him to his soldiers, to be crucified and these soldiers took Jesus out into the Prætorium, or common hall, and there in the presence of the whole band of soldiers they shamefully mocked Him. They took off His spotless garment and clad Him in purple. They put a reed in His hand to represent a sceptre. They platted a crown of thorns and put this on His brow. They spit upon Him, They smote Him. They mockingly hailed Him as a King. And all this to the One who had lived a pure, holy, unspotted life! Who had come into the world to redeem it! The One who was the long-looked-for Messiah of these same Jews!

Pilate still felt anxious to release Jesus and was still in hopes that the Jews would permit him to do so—so he went forth to them again and said:

"Behold, I bring him forth to you, that ye may know that I find no fault in him."

Jesus, clad in purple robes, now stained with blood from His lacerated back, (because of the cruel scourging), and His brow pierced by the crown of cruel thorns, came out and stood before them, and Pilate, hoping to excite their sympathy said to the Jews as he pointed to Jesus:

"Behold the man!"

Had there been one in that crowd who loved Him, that one would have seen in His face a look of tenderest compassion. It was the same beautiful face the sight of which had thrilled so many. There was no look of revenge or of hatred. It was rather, a look of love even for these wicked Jews. A look that told of a heart that was almost broken because of the sin of men. But the hard-hearted chief priests and scribes and others saw none of this. The hatred in their wicked hearts had blinded them. They only shouted the louder:

"Away with him, away with him, crucify him."

During all this time, our two young men had been in the home of the uncle. These events did not cover as much time as one might at first suppose. The betrayal occurred on the evening that ushered in the sixth day of the week, and all the events referred to, occurred either during that night or during the morning of the sixth day.

Just about the hour when Jesus was scourged, Bar-elah had occasion to go forth from the house, on an errand for Eliab who was busy helping his uncle. The arrest and trial of Jesus was by this time the talk of the street. It seemed to be in everybody's mouth. Little groups of men were gathered in the shops and bazaars and upon the street corners, all discussing these events. Bar-elah could hardly believe his ears. He was almost beside himself. Could all this be true? "I must hasten to Eliab," said he to himself. Just at that moment he heard a scribe say to a Pharisee:

"They're going to crucify him."

"Crucify Jesus?" asked Bar-elah of one who also heard what the scribe said.

"That's what he said," was the blunt response.

Bar-elah could stand no more. His heart was deeply touched.

"Oh what will my Eliab say! Jesus to be crucified! The pure, the holy one!" said he to himself as he hastened, yes, as he ran to his friend. He burst into the house. Eliab was alone.

"Eliab, Eliab," began Bar-elah all excited, "they've arrested the Christ, gave him a hasty trial last night, took him before Pilate, and he has delivered him to be crucified."

"Oh Elah!" was all Eliab could say as he looked into the eyes of his Elah. "My Jesus, my Christ! What an outrage! Oh that men knew Him!"

"Come with me Eliab," said Bar-elah as he took Eliab by the arm and the two went forth into the street.

"Oh yes, Eliab, I heard that Judas, the one who betrayed Jesus repented of his sin, took the thirty pieces of silver to the priests, confessed that he had betrayed innocent blood and then went out and hanged himself."

Eliab's face brightened a little.

"He ought to hang himself the wicked scoundrel," said Eliab.

CHAPTER XIV.

JUST as Bar-elah and Eliab came in view of the Prætorium, they saw an immense crowd moving along the street.

"Can it be Elah, that they are going to carry out their wicked plot this soon?" asked Eliab.

"I shouldn't wonder," answered Bar-elah, "they have seemed so determined that he should die."

The two stood still a moment. From where they were they could look down on the multitude as it came towards them.

"Oh, Eliab, there he is, there he is carrying a large cross," said Bar-elah grasping Eliab's hand. "Look."

And Eliab did look and his eyes fell upon the person of his divine Lord.

"Oh Elah!" sighed Eliab. "But do you not suppose He will deliver Himself out of their hands Elah?"

And as Bar-elah thought of the times when Jesus had escaped from them, his face brightened, and he said:

"I hope so, Eliab, I hope so."

People came from every direction and joined the multitude. Bar-elah and Eliab went with them. Yes there was Jesus, in the midst of the throng, bearing the cross on which He was to be crucified. Some of the multitude were weeping, some were shouting, some hardly knew what to do. Jesus had not gone far, however, before the soldiers took the cross from Him and compelled one named Simon, to bear it.

The multitude reached the City gate. It had by this time become very large. The soldiers led Jesus, and the two malefactors who were taken to be crucified with Him, to Golgotha, which by interpretation means, the place of a skull. Bar-elah and Eliab watched every movement. The soldiers made Simon lay the cross upon the ground. They stripped Jesus of His garments. Then they laid Him upon the cross.

"Will He submit to their cruelty Elah?" asked Eliab, almost terrified at the sight.

"It looks as though he will Eliab," responded Bar-elah.

The soldiers took great spikes and drove one through each hand and one through each foot. Every blow of the hammer as the nails were driven through the living flesh of the Christ, seemed to strike terror to the heart of each young man.

"O Elah, I can't stand this, it's such an outrage! Oh to think they are crucifying my Master and here I am and can't do anything!" sobbed Eliab. Bar-elah was silent. He quietly drew Eliab closer to him.

The cross was lifted into place, and as it was being lifted the two boys caught a glimpse of the face of Jesus. Did it show traces of anger and of hatred? Oh, no. Never did a face shine brighter than this. In every line, love and compassion was to be seen, mingled with the evidences of great physcial suffering.

Upon the cross, over the head of Jesus, Pilate caused this superscription to be placed:

"JESUS OF NAZARETH THE KING OF THE JEWS."

This was written in Hebrew, in Latin and in Greek, so that all who passed by might read. The soldiers parted His garments among them.

Bar-elah and Eliab and the disciples immediately about them, made a move towards the cross. The same thought seemed to be in the minds of all—that of attempting to release Jesus. Very little attention was paid to the two crucified with Him for these were malefactors and were guilty—but all who knew the Christ knew Him to be innocent.

Just as the boys came to the cross Jesus was

heard to speak. It was hardly more than a whisper, but the boys heard it, and, oh of what love those words told! It was a prayer for His murderers:

"Father forgive them for they know not what they do."

Bar-elah looked at Eliab and then into the face of Jesus. The thief on the cross at His side is now heard to speak but all the boys heard was the reply given him by Jesus:

"To-day shalt thou be with me in Paradise."

All this time the soldiers and Jews who had not believed on Him stood about wagging their heads and mocking Him—telling Him to save Himself, to come down from the cross, and so on.

Bar-elah and Eliab for a moment stood looking into the face of Jesus and then Bar-elah, slipping his arm about Eliab said, as his eyes were fixed on Jesus:

"My Master and my Redeemer."

Eliab's heart bounded for he knew his friend had received the Christ as his own Lord.

"Eliab, He is the Christ of God, I know. I can see it in His face. I can hear it in the words He speaks. I know He is the Lord," whispered Bar-elah.

Eliab was so overcome with joy he could say nothing more than——"dear Elah, my brother disciple."

John the beloved disciple of Jesus stood with Mary the mother of the Christ, at the foot of the cross. To Mary Jesus said, referring to His beloved John:

"Woman, behold thy son!" and to John He said:

"Behold thy mother!"

Suddenly it began to grow very dark although it was only about the sixth hour of the day.

What could it all mean! Eliab remembered that Jesus had said of Himself:

"I am the light of the world."

Could it be that now as He was dying, the light was going out? Surely it seemed so.

Our two young men were so astonished they did not know what to do.

"If the end of all things is at hand Eliab, we might as well be right here near our Jesus, as any other place," said Bar-elah. Eliab thought so too.

By the time the sixth hour arrived, the darkness was very dense. No night had ever seemed as dark. It continued until about the ninth hour.

"Oh Elah, how the Christ must suffer!" said Eliab. His thoughts were not so much upon the dense darkness and the surroundings as upon Jesus.

"Eli, Eli, lama sabachthani!" It was Jesus who spoke. He cried with a loud voice. Both boys understood the words perfectly. They were these: "My God, My God, why hast thou forsaken me?"

Then all was quiet until Jesus spoke again. He simply said:

"I thirst," and those who stood near gave Him a drink of vinegar.

"He can't last much longer, Eliab. His sufferings are almost at an end," said Bar-elah.

"It is finished," said Jesus softly and then, as His head fell upon His breast:

"Father, into thy hands I commend my spirit"——and He was dead.

"Oh Elah can it be that our Master is dead? Oh how cruel"——and Eliab was joined in his weeping by stalwart Bar-elah.

Suddenly the earth began to shake and the rocks where the boys stood were rent. The terrified people ran in every direction——but our two young men and a little company of faithful ones still lingered at the foot of the cross. A centurion who stood near was heard to say:

"Truly this man was the Son of God."

Bar-elah and Eliab soon left the scene of the crucifixion and went to the home of the Uncle. They were sad at heart because of the death of the One whom now, both of them loved. As they went along the street of the City one after another of the rabble was heard to cast all manner of slurs at Jesus and His disciples——for now they felt that they had truly put an end to the humble Nazarene.

Slowly the little company left Golgotha. The soldiers broke the legs of the two malefactors, but finding that Jesus was dead, they passed Him by. One of them, however, thrust his spear into the side of His body and blood and water flowed forth.

The Sabbath was drawing near. It was the great day of the feast—a high day. Joseph of Arimathæa, one of the disciples of Jesus got permission from Pilate to bury the body of Jesus, so he and Nicodemus, after the body was removed from the cross, prepared it for burial, and laid it in a new sepulchre in the garden close to the place where He was crucified. A great stone was rolled before the door of the tomb.

The chief priests and Pharisees remembered that Jesus had said: "After three days I will rise again," so they got Pilate to set a guard over the tomb, and put his seal upon it, "Lest," as they said, "his disciples come by night, and steal him away, and say unto the people, He is risen from the dead."

That Sabbath day was a quiet one for Barelah and Eliab. Although it was a high day and there was great rejoicing, the boys could not help but feel sad when they remembered the cruel, ignominious death that their Master had suffered, and yet there was a peace within the soul of each that was not disturbed at all——the peace of God given them through faith in Jesus the Christ.

"Let us go home to-morrow with the folks, Elah," said Eliab that night after they had retired. "We might as well, Eliab," said Bar-elah.

* * * * *

A day or two after Bar-elah and Eliab had returned to their home town, they went down to the banks of the Jordan, and sat in the same spot where we first saw them. Before long some one was heard approaching. He was chanting a psalm of thanksgiving. The trees hid him from view.

"It sounds like Eliphaz," said Bar-elah, "he seems happy. I wonder what the latest news from Jerusalem, is."

It was Eliphaz.

"Good news for you my friends," were the first words he spoke when he came in sight of them. "The Lord is risen from the dead and has appeared unto several of His disciples."

"Oh Eliphaz, can it be true?" said Bar-elah.

"Yes," continued Eliphaz as he took a seat near the two boys, "and I hastened to you to tell you all about it."

Both boys were eager to hear it all. Eliphaz continued:

"It seems that early on the first day of the

week, some of the women who believed on Jesus went to the sepulchre to anoint His body. When they got to the tomb they found the stone rolled away to one side. When they looked within the sepulchre, the body of Jesus was not there, but they saw a young man—an angel—of most beautiful countenance and appearance, sitting on one side. He told them that Jesus was risen and that He had gone into Galilee and there they might see Him.

"The women left in great haste to tell all these things to His disciples, but as they were going, Jesus Himself met them and spoke to them. He bade them go and tell His brethren to go into Galilee where they would see Him. The women went as He bade them. The disciples did not believe them at first, but Peter and John, two of the eleven ran with haste to the sepulchre and found all things as the women had said.

"Afterwards Jesus appeared unto Mary Magdalene and to Peter and then to two disciples as they journeyed to Emmaus. Then to the eleven as they sat together breaking bread. The doors were all shut but suddenly He was seen in their midst and brake bread with them."

The countenances of both boys beamed with delight at this blessed, this glorious news.

"Oh Elah," said Eliab, "how I wish we all might see Him!"

"So do I, Eliab," said his friend.

Several days later Eliab and Bar-elah started with Eliphaz for Capernaum. As they went through Galilee they overtook quite a company of the disciples of Jesus who were going to a certain mountain where they expected to meet Jesus. The three young men joined the company. When they reached the mountain, they found nearly five hundred others. Suddenly Jesus appeared unto them.

"Rabboni," said both our young men as their eyes rested upon Him.

"My Lord! my risen Redeemer," said Bar-elah. And as they looked upon His pierced hands and feet and side and then into His face, both boys were thrilled.

Bar-elah, Eliab and Eliphaz the next day reached Capernaum. Some time afterwards the three were sitting together on the house-top, when the grandfather of Eliphaz came up to them.

"I have just heard," said he, "that Jesus of Nazareth while walking out to Bethany with his disciples, was suddenly lifted up and carried away from them and received into heaven."

"Oh Eliab," said Bar-elah after he and his companion had retired for the night, "my dear friend Eliab, I'm so glad that I went with you when you undertook to follow Jesus, and that I too have accepted Him as my Redeemer."

"And I'm glad too my dear Elah," was the response from Eliab.

"To tell you the truth Eliab," Bar-elah said, "I felt drawn towards Him from the very first. I could see from the first that there was something more than human about Him. And what a wonderfully beautiful life His was! What an evidence of divinity was given in His death! And what glory shone from His face as we saw Him on the mountain!"

"Yes Elah, it was all so wonderful, And to think that you and I have known Him and received Him. Oh how blessed!"

There was in the heart of each boy that peace which Jesus had said He would give to those who were His disciples—it was "the peace of God, which passeth all understanding."

THE END.

www.ingramcontent.com/pod-product-compliance
Lightning Source LLC
Chambersburg PA
CBHW021936160426
43195CB00011B/1114